AN ILLUSTRATED GUIDE TO
BOMBERS
OF WORLD WAR II

2

AN ILLUSTRATED GUIDE TO
BOMBERS
OF WORLD WAR II

Bill Gunston

Published by Arco Publishing, Inc.
NEW YORK

A Salamander Book

Published by
Arco Publishing, Inc.,
219 Park Avenue South,
New York
N.Y. 10003,
United States of America.

© 1980 by Salamander Books Ltd.,
27 Old Gloucester Street,
London WC1N 3AF,
United Kingdom

All rights reserved.

Library of Congress catalog card
number 80-67628

ISBN 0-668-05094-2

All correspondence concerning the
content of this volume should be
addressed to Salamander Books Ltd.

This book may not be sold
outside the USA and Canada.

Contents

Aircraft are arranged in alphabetical order of manufacturers' names,
followed by the countries of origin.

Armstrong Whitworth
  A.W.38 Whitley   UK 8
Avro 679 Manchester   UK 10
Avro 683 Lancaster   UK 12
Bloch 174   France 18
Boeing B-17 Fortress   USA 20
Boeing B-29
  Superfortress   USA 24
Bristol Type 152
  Beaufort   UK 26
Bristol Type 142
  Blenheim   UK 30
Cant Z.1007 Alcione   Italy 34
Caproni Ca 133   Italy 36
Caproni Ca 135   Italy 38
Caproni Ca 309-316   Italy 38
Consolidated Vultee
  B-24 Liberator   US 42
Consolidated Vultee
  B-32 Dominator   US 44
Dornier Do 17   Germany 46

Dornier Do 217   Germany 50
Douglas A-26 Invader   US 56
Douglas DB-7 Family   US 54
Fairey Battle   UK 58
Farman F222   France 60
Fiat B.R. 20 Cicogna   Italy 60
Focke-Wulf Fw 200
  Condor   Germany 64
Fokker C.X   Netherlands 66
Handley Page Halifax   UK 68
Handley Page Hampden UK 72
Heinkel He 111   Germany 76
Heinkel He 177 Greif
                   Germany 82
Ilyushin Il-4   Soviet Union 84
Junkers Ju 86   Germany 86
Junkers Ju 188   Germany 88
Junkers Ju 290   Germany 90
Kawasaki Ki-48 ''Lily''
                     Japan 92

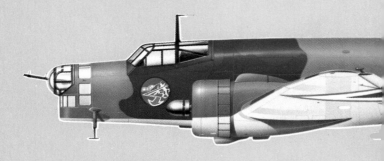

Credits

Author: Bill Gunston, former
Technical Editor of *Flight
International*, Assistant Compiler of
Jane's All the World's Aircraft,
contributor to many Salamander
illustrated reference books.

Editor: Ray Bonds
Designer: Lloyd Martin

Color and line drawings:
© Pilot Press Ltd.
Photographs: The publishers wish to
thank all the official international
governmental archives, aircraft and
systems manufacturers and private
collections who have supplied
photographs for this book.

Printed in Belgium by
Henri Proost et Cie.

Lockheed Model 414
  Hudson   US **92**
Lockheed PV-1/B-34
  Ventura   US **96**
Martin 167 Maryland   US **98**
Martin 179 B-26
  Marauder   US **100**
Martin 187 Baltimore   US **104**
Mitsubishi G3M "Nell"
                         Japan **106**
Mitsubishi G4M "Betty"
                         Japan **108**
Mitsubishi Ki-21 "Sally"
                         Japan **110**
Mitsubishi Ki-30 "Ann"
                         Japan **114**
Mitsubishi Ki-67 Hiryu
  "Peggy"   Japan **116**
Nakajima Ki-49 Donryu
  "Helen"   Japan **118**
North American NA-62
  B-25 Mitchell   US **120**

Petlyakov Pe-2 and Pe-3
                 Soviet Union **126**
Petlyakov Pe-8
                 Soviet Union **130**
PZL P.23 and 43 Karaś
                     Poland **132**
PZL P.37 Los   Poland **134**
Savoia-Marchetti S.M. 79
  Sparviero   Italy **136**
Savoia-Marchetti S.M. 81
  Pipistrello   Italy **140**
SNCASE LeO 451   France **140**
Short S.29 Stirling   UK **142**
Tupolev SB-2   Soviet Union **146**
Tupolev TB-3   Soviet Union **148**
Tupolev Tu-2   Soviet Union **150**
Vickers Wellesley   UK **152**
Vickers-Armstrong
  Wellington   UK **154**

Introduction

Nearly all the bombers of World War II were of types first flown back in the 1930s, and many had seen action in Spain and other wars of the period. Yet nearly all were monoplanes of all-metal stressed skin construction, notable exceptions being the mixed metal/wood/fabric Italian bombers, and the fabric-covered "geodetic" Wellington.

In Spain the new crop of German bombers, such as the Do 17 and He 111, proved very effective when defended by three hand-aimed rifle-calibre machine guns, but this was woefully inadequate over Britain. More guns were hastily added in an ill-planned way, but, though German guns were outstanding, the Germans completely failed to get a really good heavy bomber into service and the poor old He 111 soldiered on to the end. By far the best Luftwaffe all-rounder was the Ju 88, described in a companion volume on fighter and attack aircraft. Its immediate predecessor on the drawing board, the Ju 87 "Stuka" dive bomber (also in the companion volume), proved effective only when complete mastery of the aid had been gained.

In contrast, the policy of the US Army Air Force was to send vast formations of heavies across hostile territory in daylight, fighting their way to a distant target which would then be bombed with precision in a way that was very difficult to do at night. Using the high-flying and well-defended (but slow) B-17 and B-24, the courageous Americans succeeded in this objective, but only after suffering severe losses in bitter fighting that at the same time sapped at the entire defensive strength of the once-

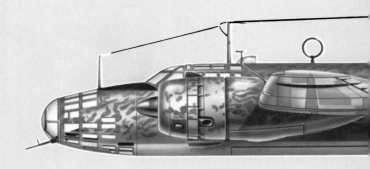

mighty Luftwaffe. As early as 1938 Boeing had begun work on a much more advanced bomber, with pressurized crew compartments and – despite wing-loading roughly double the norm – unparalleled altitude performance, with the ability to cruise at about 35,000 feet. This great bomber became the B-29 Superfortress, and it not only introduced such advanced features as electrically signalled remote-control turrets mounting 13 heavy-calibre guns but it dramatically upgraded the whole level of aviation technology. It was copied in the Soviet Union, and in 1952 the RAF was glad to have second-hand examples to equip Bomber Command.

The most numerous British bomber was the versatile Wellington, but the main weight of the saturation night attacks was carried by the Lancaster, an excellent trucking system but one bristling with defence except where it mattered (underneath, where there was not even a small porthole to see the formating night fighters). The Soviet Union devoted little effort to its chief heavy bomber, the Pe-8, and concentrated instead on the twin-engined Il-4 and Pe-2, later joined by the outstanding Tu-2. Italy's odd trimotors were skilfully flown but obsolescent, and nothing adequate followed to replace them. In Japan the impressive G8N never got into action, the G4M was too lightly built and prone to catch fire, and if anything the nation's offensive capability declined steadily from 1942 onwards. In late 1944 deliberate suicide missions suggested the war was already lost.

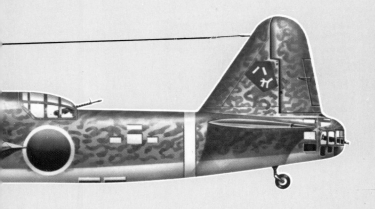

Armstrong Whitworth A.W.38 Whitley

Whitley I to VIII (data for V)

Origin: Sir W. G. Armstrong Whitworth Aircraft.
Type: Five-seat heavy bomber.
Engines: Two 1,145hp Rolls-Royce Merlin X vee-12 liquid-cooled.
Dimensions: Span 84ft 0in (25·6m); length 70ft 6in (21·5m); height 15ft 0in (4·57m).
Weights: Empty 19,330lb (8768kg); maximum 33,500lb (15,196kg).
Performance: Maximum speed 222mph (357km/h); cruising speed, about 185mph (297km/h); initial climb 800ft (244m)/min; service ceiling from 17,600–21,000ft (5400–6400m); range with maximum bomb load 470 miles (756km); range with 3,000lb (1361kg) bombs 1,650 miles (2650km).
Armament: One 0·303 in Vickers K in nose turret; four 0·303 in Brownings in tail turret; up to 7,000lb (3175kg) bombs in cells in fuselage and inner wings.
History: First flight (prototype) 17 March 1936; first delivery (Mk I) January 1937; first flight (Mk V) December 1938; first delivery (Mk V) August 1939; production termination June 1943.
User: UK (RAF BOAC).

Development: Designed to Specification B.3/34, this heavy bomber was at least an all-metal monoplane with retractable landing gear, but the original Mk I was still primitive. Its thick wing, which in the first batch had no dihedral, was set at a marked positive incidence, so that at normal cruising speeds the long slab-sided Whitley flew in a characteristic nose-down attitude. Powered by 795hp Armstrong Siddeley Tiger IX radials, the Mk I was soon replaced by the Mk II, and then by the III with the 920hp

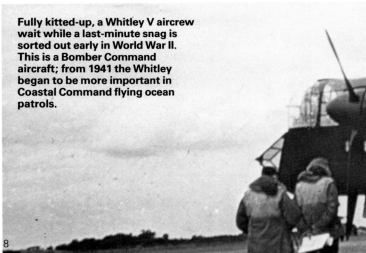

Fully kitted-up, a Whitley V aircrew wait while a last-minute snag is sorted out early in World War II. This is a Bomber Command aircraft; from 1941 the Whitley began to be more important in Coastal Command flying ocean patrols.

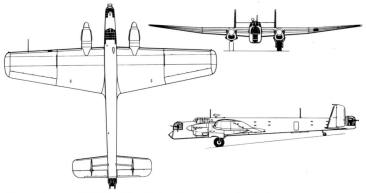

Above: Typical Whitley V with landing gear extended.

Tiger VIII. In 1938 production switched to the greatly improved Mk IV, with Merlin engines and a power-driven rear turret mounting four machine guns. The Mk IVA had a more powerful Merlin, and this was retained in the Mk V which was 15in longer and had straight-edged fins. AWA made 1,466 Whitley Vs, the last in June 1943, and also delivered 146 longer-range GR.VIII patrol aircraft with ASV radar for Coastal Command. Whitleys bore the brunt of long leaflet raids, starting on the first night of the war. On 19 March 1940 Whitleys dropped the first bombs to fall on Germany since 1918, and during the next two years these tough and capable aircraft made missions as far as Turin and Pilsen, often in terrible conditions, highlighting deficiencies in navigation and equipment the hard way. Coastal's first U-boat kill was U-206, sunk by a Whitley VII in November 1941. From 1942 the Whitley served mainly as a trainer for paratroops, as a glider tug and with 100 Group as a carrier of experimental or special-purpose radars and countermeasures. Total production was 1,737.

Left: This Whitley V served in the early part of the war with 102 Sqn. It took part in many leaflet raids, minelaying sorties and early missions to bomb targets in Germany and northern Italy.

Avro 679 Manchester

679 Manchester I and IA

Origin: A. V. Roe Ltd, Chadderton.
Type: Heavy bomber.
Engines: Two Rolls-Royce Vulture I 24-cylinder X-form, rated at 1,760hp but in fact derated to 1,480–1,500hp.
Dimensions: Span 90ft 1in (27·46m); length 70ft 0in (21·34m); height 19ft 6in (5·94m).
Weights: Empty 31,200lb (14,152kg); maximum 56,000lb but in fact never authorised above 50,000lb (22,680kg).
Performance: Maximum speed (typical) 250mph (402km/h); service ceiling (42,000lb) 19,500ft (5852m); range with maximum bomb load 1,200 miles (1930km).
Armament: Eight 0·303in Browning in power turrets in nose (2), mid-upper (2) and tail (4); internal fuselage bay accommodating bomb load up to 10,350lb (4695kg).
History: First flight 25 July 1939; service delivery November 1940; withdrawal from production November 1941.
User: UK (RAF).

Development: Rolls-Royce's decision in 1935 to produce a very powerful engine by fitting two sets of Peregrine cylinder-blocks to one crankcase (the lower pair being inverted, to give an X arrangement) prompted the Air Ministry to issue specification P.13/36 for a twin-engined heavy bomber of unprecedented capability. Handley Page changed to four Merlins (see Halifax) but Avro produced the Manchester with the Vulture engine. In most respects it was the best of all the new heavy bombers, but the engine was grossly down on power, and had to be derated further because of extreme unreliability. Originally the Manchester had two fins; in the production Mk I a fixed central fin was added, and the bulk of the 209 delivered had two larger fins (no central fin) and were designated IA. So hopeless was the engine situation that the plans to build Manchesters at Armstrong Whitworth and Fairey were cancelled, and Metropolitan-Vickers stopped at No 32. Avro went on until the vastly superior Lancaster could take over, the first batches of Lancasters having Manchester fuselages with a row of small windows along each side.

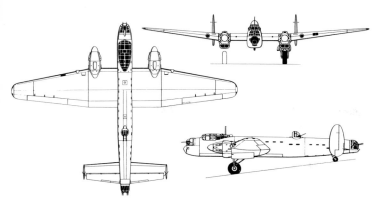

Above: Mk 1A with two enlarged fins on increased-span tailplane.

Above: L7516, ''S-Sugar'' of 207 Sqn, the first unit to receive the Manchester in November 1940. This aircraft was a Mk IA.

Below: L7284 was the ninth production Manchester I, the original model with a central fin. It was photographed in 1940 soon after delivery to 207 Sqn. Later, fuselage sides were black (above).

Avro 683 Lancaster
683 Lancaster I to MR.7 (data for I)

Origin: A. V. Roe Ltd; also Armstrong Whitworth, Austin Motors, Metropolitan-Vickers and Vickers-Armstrongs, UK, and Victory Aircraft, Canada.
Type: Seven-seat heavy bomber.
Engines: Four 1,460hp Rolls-Royce or Packard Merlin 20 or 22 (Mk II only: four 1,650hp Bristol Hercules VI, 14 cylinder two-row, sleeve-valve radials).
Dimensions: Span 102ft 0in (31·1m); length 69ft 4in (21·1m); height 19ft 7in (5·97m).
Weights: Empty 36,900lb (16,705kg); loaded 68,000lb (30,800kg); overload with 22,000lb bomb 70,000lb (31,750kg).
Performance: Maximum speed 287mph (462km/h) at 11,500ft (3500m); cruising speed 210mph (338km/h); climb at maximum weight to 20,000ft (6095m) 41 minutes; service ceiling 24,500ft (7467m); range with 14,000lb (6350kg) bombs 1,660 miles (2675km).
Armament: Nose and dorsal turrets (Mk II also ventral) with two 0·303in Brownings (some, including Mk VII, had Martin dorsal turret with two 0·5in), tail turret with four 0·303 in Brownings, 33ft 0in (10·06m) bomb bay carrying normal load of 14,000lb (6350kg) or 22,000lb (9979kg) bomb with modification.
History: First flight 9 January 1941; service delivery (for test and training) September 1941; last delivery from new 2 February 1946.
Users: Australia, Canada, New Zealand, Poland, UK (RAF, BOAC).

Development: Undoubtedly one of the major influences on World War II, and one of the greatest aircraft of history, the "Lanc" came about because of the failure of its predecessor. In September 1936 the Air Staff issued specification P.13/36 for a twin-engined bomber of exceptional size and capability to be powered by two of the very powerful engines then under development: the Rolls-Royce Vulture 24-cylinder X engine was preferred. Handley Page switched to four Merlins with the Halifax, but A. V. Roe adhered to the big-twin formula and the first Type 679 Manchester flew on 25 July 1939. Altogether 209 Manchesters were delivered by November 1941, but the type was plagued by the poor performance and unreliability of its engine. Though it equipped eight Bomber Command squadrons, and parts of two others plus a flight in Coastal Command, the Manchester was withdrawn from service in June 1942 and survivors were scrapped.

Nevertheless the basic Manchester was clearly outstandingly good, and in 1940 the decision was taken to build a longer-span version with four Merlin engines. The first Lancaster (BT 308) flew as the Manchester III at the beginning of 1941. So outstanding was its performance that it went ▶

Below: The famous Lancaster S-Sugar now preserved in the RAF Museum at Hendon. A B.I that served with 467 Sqn, from Waddington, it completed 137 missions, thought to be a record. Unfortunately the true leader, with 140 missions, was scrapped.

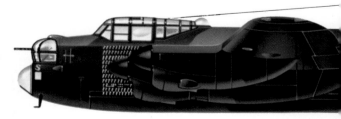

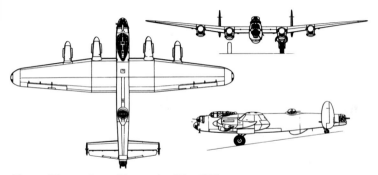

Above: Three-view of Lancaster B.I or B.III.

Below: Lancasters bombing through cloud. Bomber Command perfected many advanced methods of radio and radar navigation, target marking and blind bombing, as well as more than 17 types of ECM (electronic countermeasures) and spoofing or decoys.

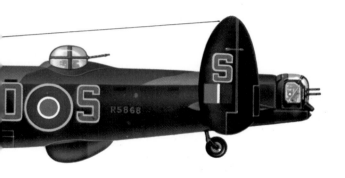

into immediate large-scale production, and Manchesters already on the line from L7527 onwards were completed as Lancasters (distinguished from later aircraft by their row of rectangular windows in the rear fuselage). Deliveries began in early 1942 to 44 Sqn at Waddington, and on 17 April 1942 a mixed force of 44 and 97 Sqns made a rather foolhardy daylight raid against the MAN plant at Augsburg, whereupon the new bomber's existence was revealed.

From then until the end of World War II Lancasters made 156,000 sorties in Europe and dropped 608,612 long tons of bombs. Total production, including 430 in Canada by Victory Aircraft, was 7,377. Of these 3,425

were Mk I and 3,039 the Mk III with US Packard-built engines. A batch of 300 was built as Mk IIs with the more powerful Bristol Hercules radial, some with bulged bomb bays and a ventral turret. The Mk I (Special) was equipped to carry the 12,000lb (5443kg) light-case bomb and the 12,000lb and 22,000lb (9979kg) Earthquake bombs, the H_2S radar blister under the rear fuselage being removed. The Mk I (FE) was equipped for Far East ▶

Below: The first unit to convert to the Lancaster was No 44 (Rhodesia) Sqn, previously equipped with Hampdens. This fine photograph of some of 44's Lancs was taken later in 1942.

operations with Tiger Force. The aircraft of 617 (Dambusters) Sqn were equipped to spin and release the Wallis skipping drum bomb. The Mk VI had high-altitude Merlins and four-blade propellers and with turrets removed served 635 Sqn and 100 Grp as a countermeasure and radar spoof carrier. Other marks served as photo-reconnaissance and maritime reconnaissance and air/sea rescue aircraft, the last MR.7 leaving RAF front-line service in February 1954.

Lancasters took part in every major night attack on Germany. They soon showed their superiority by dropping 132 long tons of bombs for each aircraft lost, compared with 56 (later 86) for the Halifax and 41 for the Stirling. They carried a heavier load of bigger bombs than any other aircraft in the European theatre. The 12,000lb AP bomb was used to sink the *Tirpitz*, and the 22,000lb weapon finally shook down the stubborn viaduct at Bielefeld in March 1945. Around Caen, Lancasters were used en masse in the battlefield close-support role, and they finished the war dropping supplies to starving Europeans and ferrying home former prisoners of war.

Right: The last of a dozen thousand-pounders is winched up into the capacious bay of a Lancaster. Behind the armourer, who is stripped to the waist, can be seen the black bulge housing the H_2S radar which Luftwaffe night fighters found a useful beacon.

Below: An inspiring sight to anyone who remembers those great days – the final assembly line at A. V. Roe's Woodford plant in 1943 (Mk is with serials in the batch JA672-JB748).

17

Bloch 174

174 A3, 175 B3 and T

Origin: SNCASO.
Type: Three-seat reconnaissance, target marker and light bomber.
Engines: Two 1,140hp Gnome-Rhône 14N 14-cylinder radials.
Dimensions: Span 58ft 9½in (17·9m); length 40ft 1½in (12·23m); height 11ft 7¾in (3·59m).
Weights: Empty 12,346lb (5600kg); maximum 15,784lb (7160kg).
Performance: Maximum speed 329mph (529km/h) at 17,060ft (5200m); cruising speed 248mph (400km/h); climb to 26,250ft (8000m) 11min; service ceiling 36,090ft (11,000m); maximum range with 880lb (400kg) bomb load 800 miles (1,450km).
Armament: Two 7·5mm MAC 1934 fixed in wings, three fixed at different angles below and to the rear, and two manually aimed from rear cockpit; internal bay for eight 110lb (50kg) bombs, wing racks for light bombs or flares (175, three 441lb or equivalent).
History: First flight (170-01) 15 February 1938; (174-01) 5 January 1939; (first production 174 A3) 5 November 1939; first delivery to combat unit (GR II/33) 19 March 1940.
Users: France (Armée de l'Air, Aéronavale, Vichy AF), Germany (Luftwaffe).

Development: Under chief designer Henri Deplante the Bloch 170 was planned as a bomber and army co-operation machine in 1936—37. As a result of indecision by the Armée de l'Air this took three years to evolve into the Bloch 174 A3 reconnaissance and target-marking aircraft, with secondary capability as a bomber. By the time production of the 174 stopped in May 1940 a total of 50 had been delivered. The first sortie was flown in March 1940 by the famed Capitaine Antoine de Saint-Exupéry. As it had an insignificant bomb load the 174 made little impact on the Blitzkrieg — it was only in 1942, in Tunisia, that the survivors were fitted to conduct shallow dive-bombing with bombs of up to 500kg (1,102lb) — but the performance and handling were so outstanding and made such a difference to the casualty-rate among squadrons equipped with the type, that the Bloch 175 was hurriedly planned as a purpose-designed bomber. Altogether 25 Bloch 175 B3s were completed before France collapsed, with more than 200 on the production line, and had France been able to resist longer the 175 would have been a potent weapon. A few 174 and 175 aircraft saw service with the Luftwaffe, but most served Vichy France in North Africa and many survived the war. Indeed the torpedo-carrying 175T remained in production for the Aéronavale until 1950.

Below: A Bloch 174 A3 serving with GR II/33 of the Vichy forces based at Tunis El Aouina in 1941-42. Some of these aircraft had engine cowlings painted in yellow/red stripes in common with many other aircraft of the Vichy forces, including US-supplied types.

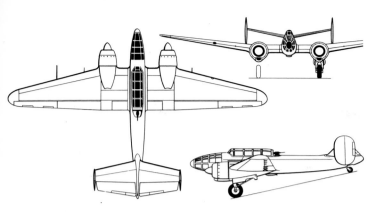

Above: Three-view of Bloch 174A3.

Above: The Bloch 174 A3 was an outstanding multi-role aircraft and, had it not been for the disastrous and defeatist political and industrial environment into which it was born, it might have made a major contribution to Allied victory. As it was, not one reached the Armée de l'Air until 19 March 1940, and the first operational sortie took place ten days later. Barely a year later the chief contribution of this machine was to provide a fully developed engine for the German Messerschmitt Me 323 Gigant cargo transport, some of which actually flew with engines, cowlings and propellers taken from Bloch 175s already completed.

Boeing B-17 Fortress

Model 299, Y1B-17 and B-17 to B-17G (basic data for G)

Origin: Boeing Airplane Company, Seattle; also built by Vega Aircraft Corporation, Burbank, and Douglas Aircraft Company, Tulsa.

Type: High-altitude bomber, with crew of six to ten.

Engines: Four 1,200hp Wright R-1820-97 (B-17C to E, R-1820-65) Cyclone nine-cylinder radials with exhaust-driven turbochargers.

Dimensions: Span 103ft 9in (31·6m): length 74ft 9in (22·8m); (B-17B, C, D) 67ft 11in; (B-17E) 73ft 10in; height 19ft 1in (5·8m); (B-17B, C, D) 15ft 5in.

Weights: Empty 32,720—35,800lb (14,855—16,200kg); (B-17B, C, D) typically 31,150lb; maximum loaded 65,600lb (29,700kg) (B-17B, C, D) 44,200—46,650lb; (B-17E) 53,000lb.

Performance: Maximum speed 287mph (462km/h); (B-17C, D) 323mph; (B-17E) 317mph; cruising speed 182mph (293km/h); (B-17C, D) 250mph; (B-17E) 210mph; service ceiling 35,000ft (10,670m); range 1,100 miles (1,760km) with maximum bomb load (other versions up to 3,160 miles with reduced weapon load).

Armament: Twin 0·5in Brownings in chin, dorsal, ball and tail turrets, plus two in nose sockets, one in radio compartment and one in each waist position. Normal internal bomb load 6,000lb (2724kg), but maximum 12,800lb (5800kg).

History: First flight (299) 28 July 1935; (Y1B-17) January 1937; first delivery (B-17B) June 1939; final delivery April 1945.

Users: UK (RAF), US (AAC/AAF, Navy).

Development: In May 1934 the US Army Air Corps issued a specification for a multi-engined anti-shipping bomber to defend the nation against enemy fleets. The answer was expected to be similar to the Martin B-10, but Boeing proposed four engines in order to carry the same bomb load faster and higher. It was a huge financial risk for the Seattle company but the resulting Model 299 was a giant among combat aircraft, with four 750hp Pratt & Whitney Hornet engines, a crew of eight and stowage for eight 600lb (272kg) bombs internally.

The service-test batch of 13 Y1B-17 adopted the Wright Cyclone engine, later versions all being turbocharged for good high-altitude performance. The production B-17B introduced a new nose and bigger rudder and flaps,

continued ▶

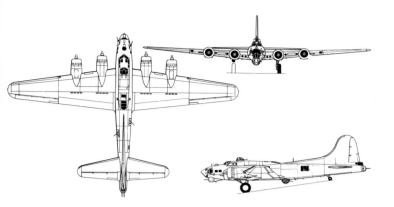

Above: Three-view of B-17G.

Above: The RAF used hundreds of Fortress IIs (B-17F) and IIIs (B-17G), the former mainly with Coastal Command with which this example was serving in 1943. The Fortress IIIs included black-painted 'specials' used by the secret 100 Group on bomber support.

Below: This B-17G-25 served in 1944 with the US 8th Army Air Force's 96th Bomb Group at Snetterton Heath. Though a much older design than the B-24 the B-17 predominated in Europe.

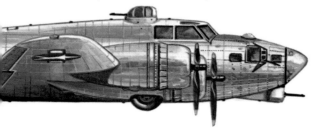

though the wing loading was conservative and an enduring characteristic of every "Fort" was sedate flying.

With the B-17C came a ventral bathtub, flush side guns, armour and self-sealing tanks. In return for combat data 20 were supplied to the RAF, which used them on a few high-altitude daylight raids with 90 Sqn of Bomber Command. It was found that the Norden sight tended to malfunction, the Browning guns to freeze at the high altitude and German fighters to attack from astern in a defensive blind spot. While surviving Fortress Is operated with Coastal and Middle East forces, the improved B-17D joined the US Army and bore the brunt of early fighting in the Pacific. But extensive combat experience led to the redesigned B-17E, with powered dorsal, ventral (ball) and tail turrets, a huge fin for high-altitude bombing accuracy and much more armour and equipment. This went into mass production by Boeing, Lockheed-Vega and Douglas-Tulsa. It was the first weapon of the US 8th Bomber Command in England and on 17 August 1942 began three gruelling years of day strategic bombing in Europe.

Soon the E gave way to the B-17F, of which 3,405 were built, with many detail improvements, including a long Plexiglas nose, paddle-blade propellers and provision for underwing racks. At the end of 1942 came the final

Below: A small portion of an 8th AF B-17G formation (from the 381st Bomb Group) with a P-51B escort fighter just beyond.

22

Above: Almost certainly taken in 1943, this photograph shows a B-17F in full battle trim, and was taken from the left waist gun position of another. Note olive-drab paint scheme.

bomber model, the B-17G, with chin turret and flush staggered waist guns. A total of 8,680 G models were made, Boeing's Seattle plant alone turning out 16 a day, and the total B-17 run amounted to 12,731. A few B-17Fs were converted to XB-40s, carrying extra defensive guns to help protect the main Bomb Groups, while at least 25 were turned into BQ-7 Aphrodite radio-controlled missiles loaded with 12,000lb of high explosive for use against U-boat shelters. Many F and G models were fitted with H_2X radar with the scanner retracting into the nose or rear fuselage, while other versions included the F-9 reconnaissance, XC-108 executive transport, CB-17 utility transport, PB-1W radar early-warning, PB-1G lifeboat-carrying air/sea rescue and QB-17 target drone. After the war came other photo, training, drone-director, search/rescue and research versions, including many used as engine and equipment testbeds. In 1970, 25 years after first flight, one of many civil Forts used for agricultural or forest-fire protection was re-engined with Dart turboprops!

Below: "Stop" waves a ground-crewman to the skipper of a red-tailed G-model on the green grass of a British base.

Boeing B-29 Superfortress
Model 345, B-29 to -29C

Origin: Boeing Airplane Company, Seattle, Renton and Wichita; also built by Bell Aircraft, Marietta, and Glenn L. Martin Company, Omaha.

Type: High-altitude heavy bomber, with crew of 10–14.

Engines: Four 2,200hp Wright R-3350-23 Duplex Cyclone 18-cylinder radials each with two exhaust-driven turbochargers.

Dimensions: Span 141ft 3in (43·05m); length 99ft (30·2m); height 27ft 9in (8·46m).

Weights: Empty 74,500lb (33,795kg); loaded 135,000lb (61,240kg).

Performance: Maximum speed 357mph (575km/h) at 30,000ft (9144m); cruising speed 290mph (467km/h); climb to 25,000ft (7620m) in 43min; service ceiling 36,000ft (10,973m); range with 10,000lb (4540kg) bombs 3,250miles (5230km).

Armament: Four GE twin-0·50in turrets above and below, sighted from nose or three waist sighting stations; Bell tail turret, with own gunner, with one 20mm cannon and twin 0·50in; internal bomb load up to 20,000lb (9072kg). Carried first two nuclear bombs. With modification, carried two 22,000lb British bombs externally under inner wings.

History: First flight 21 September 1942; (pre-production YB-29) 26 June 1943); squadron delivery July 1943; first combat mission 5 June 1944; last delivery May 1946.

User: US (AAF, Navy).

Development and mass production of the B-29, the Boeing Model 345, was one of the biggest tasks in the history of aviation. It began with a March 1938 study for a new bomber with pressurised cabin and tricycle landing gear. This evolved into the 345 and in August 1940 money was voted for two prototypes. In January 1942 the Army Air Force ordered 14 YB-29s and 500 production aircraft. By February, while Boeing engineers worked night and day on the huge technical problems, a production organisation was set up involving Boeing, Bell, North American and Fisher (General Motors). Martin came in later and, by VJ-day more than 3,000 Superforts

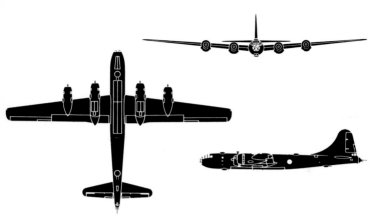

Above: Three-view of B-29 (two-gun forward dorsal turret).

had been delivered. This was a fantastic achievement because each represented five or six times the technical effort of any earlier bomber. In engine power, gross weight, wing loading, pressurisation, armament, airborne systems and even basic structure the B-29 set a wholly new standard. First combat mission was flown by the 58th Bomb Wing on 5 June 1944, and by 1945 20 groups from the Marianas were sending 500 B-29s at a time to flatten and burn Japan's cities. (Three aircraft made emergency landings in Soviet territory, and Tupolev's design bureau put the design into production as the Tu-4 bomber and Tu-70 transport.) The -29C had all guns except those in the tail removed, increasing speed and altitude. After the war there were 19 variants of B-29, not including the Washington B.I supplied to help the RAF in 1950–58.

Below: Two of the first production B-29s, painted olive drab on upper and side surfaces. All subsequent B-29s were delivered unpainted. It was a B-29, "Enola Gay", that dropped the first atomic bomb, on Hiroshima.

Bristol Type 152 Beaufort
Beaufort I to VIII

Origin: Bristol Aeroplane Company; also made by Department of Aircraft Production, Fishermen's Bend, Australia.

Type: Four-seat torpedo bomber.

Engines: Two 1,130hp Bristol Taurus VI 14-cylinder sleeve-valve radials (most other marks, two 1,200hp Pratt & Whitney Twin Wasp).

Dimensions: Span 57ft 10in (17·63m); length 44ft 2in (13·46m); height 14ft 3in (4·34m).

Weights: Empty 13,107lb (5945kg); loaded 21,230lb (9629kg).

Performance: Maximum speed 260mph (418km/h) clean, 225mph (362km/h) with torpedo; service ceiling 16,500ft (5030m); range 1,600 miles (2575km).

Armament: Various, but typically two 0·303in Vickers K in dorsal turret and one fixed forward-firing in left wing, plus one 0·303in Browning in remote-control chin blister. Alternatively four 0·303in Brownings in wing, two Brownings manually aimed from beam windows and (Mk II) twin Brownings in dorsal turret (final 140 Australian Mk VIII, two 0·50in Brownings in dorsal turret). One 18in torpedo semi-external to left of centreline or bomb load of 2,000lb (907kg).

History: First flight 15 October 1938; first delivery October 1939; first flight of Australian aircraft (Mk V) August 1941; last delivery (Australia) August 1944.

Users: Australia, Turkey, UK.

Development: Derived from the Blenheim, the torpedo-carrying Beaufort was inevitably heavier because the Air Staff demanded a crew of four. Performance on Mercury engines was inadequate and, after studying an installation of the sleeve-valve Perseus, the choice fell on the Taurus, an extremely neat two-row engine only 46in in diameter. A clever installation was schemed for this but it overheated and various engine troubles held the programme back in the early days, but 22 and 42 Sqns of Coastal Command were fully operational by August 1940. As well as laying hundreds of mines they bombed the battlecruiser *Scharnhorst*, torpedoed the *Gneisenau* and sank numerous smaller ships. In 1939 plans were laid for Beaufort production in Australia and, because of the difficulty of supplying engines from Britain, the Australian Mks V–VIII had Twin Wasp engines, most of them made in Australia. A large batch of British Beauforts (Mk II) had this engine, but a Merlin-Beaufort was abandoned and from No 165 the Mk II reverted to later models of Taurus. The total built was 2,080, including 700 built in Australia for duty in the Southwest Pacific. Australian models had a bigger fin and progressed through four series with different equipment, ending with transport and trainer versions. The finest RAAF missions were against Japanese fleets at Normanby Island, in the Timor Sea and around New Guinea and the Solomons.

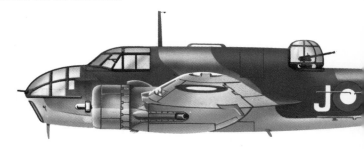

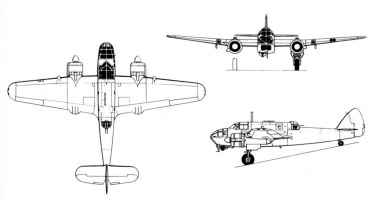

Above: Three-view of Beaufort I Series II with trailing edge extensions and rearward-firing barbette under the nose.

Below: One of the first Beaufort Is to go into operational service was this machine from 42 Sqn, RAF Coastal Command. By 1942 such aircraft had been repainted in the deep sea grey and white colour scheme, while many Beauforts had been sent to the Meditterranean and other overseas theatres. Another change was the addition of semicircular trailing-edge plates as shown in the three-view above.

Left: Australia's biggest wartime production programme of combat aircraft concerned the Beaufort, though in versions slightly different from those built in Britain. All were powered by Pratt & Whitney Twin Wasp engines, and the vast majority were Beaufort VIIIs, one of which is depicted here serving with (probably) 86 Sqn of the RAAF. Features included an improved turret, larger fin and rudder and ASV radar.

continued ▶

Little colour photography was possible in Britain during World War II because such film was virtually unobtainable. This shot shows Beaufort Is of 217 Sqn armed with torpedoes, in 1940 markings. Later, Coastal Command aircraft were grey/white.

Parked in one of the blast pens built at Luqa airport from the bombed buildings of Malta, this Beaufort is a Twin Wasp-powered Mk II. It is probably serving with RAF No 86 Sqn, which took over in Malta when 217 Sqn was posted to Burma.

Bristol Type 142 Blenheim

Types 142 M, 149 and 160 Blenheim/Bisley/ Bolingbroke (data for Blenheim IVL)

Origin: Bristol Aeroplane Company; also made by A. V. Roe, Rootes Securities and Canadian Vickers Ltd.

Type: Three-seat light bomber (IF, IVF, fighter versions).

Engines: Two 920hp Bristol Mercury XV (I, Bolingbroke I, II, 840hp Mercury VIII; Bolingbroke IV series, 750–920hp Twin Wasp Junior, Cyclone or Mercury XX; Blenheim V, 950hp Mercury XXX).

Dimensions: Span 56ft 4in (17·17m) (V, 56ft 1in); length 42ft 9in (13m) (I, 39ft 9in; Bolingbroke III, 46ft 3in; V, 43ft 11in); height 12ft 10in (3·91m) (Bolingbroke III, 18ft).

Weights: Empty 9,790lb (4441kg) (I, Bolingbroke III, 8,700lb; V, 11,000lb); loaded 14,400lb (6531kg) (I, 12,250lb; Bolingbrokes 13,400lb; V, 17,000lb).

Performance: Maximum speed 266mph (428km/h); (I) 285mph; (early IV) 295mph; (Bolingbrokes and V) 245–260mph; initial climb 1,500ft (457m)/min (others similar); service ceiling 31,500ft (9600m) (others similar except Bolingbroke III, 26,000ft); range 1,950 miles (3138km); (I) 1,125 miles; (Bolingbrokes) 1,800 miles; (V) 1,600 miles.

Armament: One 0·303in Vickers K in nose, two 0·303in Brownings in FN.54 chin turret and two 0·303in Brownings in dorsal turret; (I) single fixed Browning and single Vickers K in dorsal turret; (IF, IVF) four fixed Brownings under fuselage; bomb load 1,000lb (454kg) internal (non-standard aircraft had underwing 500lb racks).

History: First flight (Type 142) 12 April 1935; (142M Blenheim I) 25 June 1936; service delivery November 1936; termination of production (VD) June 1943; withdrawal from service (Finland) 1956.

Users: Canada, Finland, France, Greece, Jugoslavia, Lithuania, Portugal, Romania, Turkey, UK (RAF).

Development: It was the newspaper magnate Lord Rothermere who asked the Bristol company to build him a fast executive aircraft to carry a pilot and six passengers at 240mph, appreciably faster than any RAF fighter in 1934. The result was the Type 142, the first modern stressed-skin monoplane in Britain with retractable landing gear, flaps and, after a wait, imported American variable-pitch propellers. Its performance staggered even the designer, Barnwell, for on Air Ministry test it reached 307mph. The inevitable result was the Blenheim bomber, to produce which Barnwell designed a new fuselage with mid-wing and bomb bay beneath it. Pilot and nav/bomb-aimer sat in the neat glazed nose, and a part-retractable dorsal turret was added behind the wing. The Blenheim I was ordered in what were huge quantities to a company almost devoid of work. Ultimately 1,134 were built, many of which made gallant bombing raids early in the war and were then converted to IF fighter configuration (some having the AI Mk III, the first operational fighter radar in the world). The fast new bomber excited ▶

Right: L8609 was one of the Blenheim 1 bombers built in 1937–38 by Roots Securities at the giant new Shadow Factory at Speke, Liverpool. It survived the hectic campaign of 1939–40, when the Blenheim was possibly the busiest type in the RAF, and is shown as it was late in that year serving with 60 Sqn at Lahore, India.

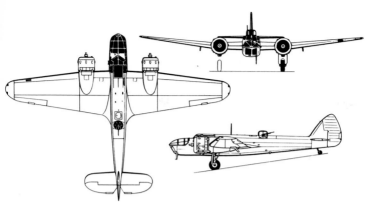

Above: Mk IV as originally delivered without under-nose gun.

Above: Almost certainly taken at Northolt shortly after the start of World War II, this line up of 604 (County of Middlesex) Sqn shows the Mk IF fighter. Soon this acquired the world's first airborne radar and operated mainly by night.

intense foreign interest and many were exported to Finland, Turkey, Jugoslavia, Lithuania, Romania and Greece. To provide a nav/bomb-aimer station ahead of the pilot the nose was then lengthened 3ft and this type was named Bolingbroke, a name retained for all the variety of Blenheims built in Canada (the Bolingbroke Mk III being a twin-float seaplane). A revised asymmetric nose was adopted for production in the speedy Mk IV, which later acquired a fighter gun pack (IVF) or a manual rear-firing chin gun (IVL), finally having a two-gun chin turret. Made by Bristol, Avro and Rootes, like the Mk I, the IV was the main combat version with the RAF, 3,297 being delivered and making many daylight missions in many theatres. The heavily armed and armoured two-seat Bisley attack aircraft did not go into production, but the three-seat equivalent did, as the Blenheim Mk V. Heavy and underpowered, the 902 VDs served in North Africa and the Far East.

Right: Blenheim IV bombers of No 139 Sqn, RAF, painted as they were at the time of the outbreak of war. On 3 September 1939, two hours after the start of hostilities, a 139 Sqn Blenheim was the first Allied aircraft to cross the German frontier.

Below: a rare colour photograph showing aircrew and ground crew of a Blenheim IV in 1941, probably about to go on one of the dangerous 'daylight sweeps' over occupied Europe. Note the asymmetric nose added to provide room for the navigator.

Cant Z.1007 Alcione

Z.1007, 1007 bis and 1018

Origin: CRDA "Cant".
Type: Four/five-seat medium bomber.
Engines: Three 1,000hp Piaggio P.XIbis RC40 14-cylinder two-row radials.
Dimensions: Span 81ft 4in (24·8m); length 60ft 4in (18·4m); height 17ft 1½in (5·22m).
Weights: Empty 19,000lb (8630kg); loaded 28,260–30,029lb (12,840–13,620kg).
Performance: Maximum speed 280mph (448km/h); initial climb 1,550ft (472m)/min; service, ceiling 26,500ft (8100m); range 800 miles (1280km) with maximum bombs, 3,100 miles (4989km) with maximum fuel.
Armament: (First 25) four 7·7mm Breda-SAFAT machine guns in dorsal turret, two beam hatches and ventral position; (remainder) as before except dorsal and ventral guns 12·7mm Breda-SAFAT; internal bomb capacity 4,410lb (2000kg); alternatively two 1,000lb (454kg) torpedoes and four bombs up to 551lb (250kg) each on underwing racks.
History: First flight May 1937; (first production aircraft) 1939; entry to service 1939.
User: Italy (RA, CB, ARSI).

continued ▶

Below: A priceless colour photograph showing twin-finned Z.1007bis bombers on a bleak airfield which may be in Sicily (it looks like North Africa but only one squadriglia briefly operated in that theatre). Single- and twin-finned Alciones operated together, and there was no distinguishing designation.

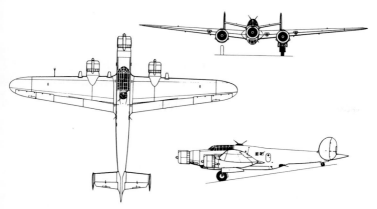

Above: Three-view of typical Z.1007bis (twin-finned version).

Below: Again it is the twin-finned model that forms the subject of this painting, the unit being the 230a Squadriglia, 950 Gruppo. Despite its wooden construction this bomber stood up well to the heat of Libya and the bitter cold of the Russian front.

Development: A famous Italian naval yard, the Cantieri Monfalcone (Trieste), entered the aircraft construction business in 1923, forming a subsidiary called Cantieri Riuniti dell' Adriatico (always shortened to Cant). Their first products were seaplanes and flying boats and the most important of these was the three-engined Z.506B Airone (Heron) twin-float seaplane used in large numbers in World War II. Designer Filippo Zappata then produced a landplane bomber version, powered by three 840hp Isotta-Fraschini Asso inverted-vee liquid-cooled engines. Like the seaplane this new bomber, the Z.1007, was built entirely of wood. It received a generally favourable report from the Regia Aeronautica's test pilots and after modifications went into production, two other firms — Meridionali and Piaggio — later being brought in to increase rate of output. Nearly all the several hundred production Alciones (Kingfishers) were powered by the Piaggio radial engine, and this version, the Z.1007 bis, also had a longer fuselage, bigger wings and stronger landing gear. Almost half also had twin tail fins. Though easy meat for RAF fighters, Alciones were bravely operated throughout the Mediterranean, and many even served on the Russian front. Various developments culminated in the excellent twin-engined Z.1018 Leone (Lion), with metal airframe and 1,350hp engines, but few of these had been delivered when Italy surrendered in 1943.

Right: Single-finned Alciones of the 230a Squadriglia in quite tight formation at low level over cultivated but otherwise featureless terrain. The photograph is dated 1940, a year in which fewer than 90 of this type had been delivered.

Caproni Ca 133

Ca 101, 111 and 133 (data for 133)

Origin: Società Italiana Caproni.
Type: Colonial bomber and transport.
Engines: Three 450/460hp Piaggio P.VII RC14 Stella seven-cylinder radials.
Dimensions: Span 69ft 8in (21·3m); length 50ft 4¾in (15·35m); height 13ft 1in (4m).
Weights: Empty 8,598lb (3900kg); loaded 14,330lb (6500kg).
Performance: Maximum speed 174mph (280km/h); initial climb 940ft (286m)/min; service ceiling 21,325ft (6500m); range 839 miles (1350km).
Armament: One or two 7·7mm or one 12·7mm machine gun on pivoted mounting in roof at trailing edge of wing; one machine gun in sliding hatchway in floor of rear fuselage; often one 7·7mm on each side in aft window-openings; bomb load (up to 2,200lb, 1000kg) carried in internal bay and on external racks under fuselage.
History: First flight (Ca 101) 1932; (Ca 111) 1933; (Ca 133) 1935; end of production, prior to 1938.
Users: Austria, Hungary, Italy (RA).

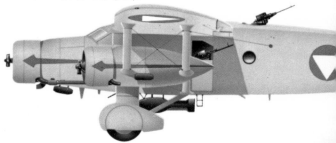

Development: As Mussolini restored "the lost colonies" and Italy forcibly built up an overseas empire, so did the need arise for "colonial" type aircraft similar to the British Wapiti and Vincent. Caproni produced the Ca 101 to meet this need, at least 200 being delivered in the early 1930s to serve as bomber, troop carrier, reconnaissance and ground attack machines and, most of all, to supply forward troops with urgent stores. Powered by three 235hp Alfa Romeo engines, it was made of robust welded steel tube with fabric covering. The Ca 111, powered by a single 950hp Isotta-Fraschini engine, gave even better service and survived the Albanian and Ethiopian campaigns to operate against Jugoslav partisans in World War II. The Ca 133 was the most important of all and many hundreds were built. When Italy entered the war in 1940 it equipped 14 Squadriglie di Bombardimento Terrestri (bomber squadrons), nearly all in East or North Africa. Though scorned by the RAF and easy meat on the ground or in the air, these versatile STOL machines worked hard and well and finished up as ambulances and transports in Libya, on the Russian Front and in Italy (on both sides after the 1943 surrender).

Left: A fully armed Ca 133 of Fliegerregiment 2 of the Austrian Air Force, one of several export customers. In the 1930s these versatile machines gave excellent service, but by the time Italy entered World War II they were outclassed. Their crews called them Vacca (cow) or Caprona (she-goat), which was a play on the name of the manufacturer. Two advanced models, the Ca 142 and 148, did not go into production.

Caproni Ca 135

Ca 135 and 135bis (data for 135bis)

Origin: Società Italiana Caproni.
Type: Five-seat medium bomber.
Engines: Two 1,000hp Piaggio P.XIbis RC40 14-cylinder two-row radials.
Dimensions: Span 61ft 8in (18·75m); length 47ft 1in (14·4m); height 11ft 2in (3·4m).
Weights: Empty 9,921lb (4500kg); loaded 18,740lb (8500kg).
Performance: Maximum speed 273mph (440km/h); initial climb 1,435ft (437m)/min; service ceiling 22,966ft (7000m); range with bomb load 746 miles (1200km).
Armament: Three Breda-SAFAT turrets, each mounting one 12·7mm or two 7·7mm guns, in nose, dorsal and ventral positions (dorsal and ventral retractable); bomb cells in fuselage and inner wings for up to 3,527lb (1600kg) weapon load.
History: First flight (135) 1 April 1935; (135bis) about November 1937.
Users: Hungary, Italy (RA).

Caproni Ca 309-316

Ca 309 Ghibli (Desert Wind), 310 Libeccio (Southwest Wind), 311 and 311M, 312 and variants, 313, 314 and variants and 316

Origin: Cantieri Aeronautici Bergamaschi; production by various other Caproni companies, mainly at Castellamare and Taliedo.
Type: (309) colonial utility, (310) utility transport, (311) light bomber, (312) bomber and torpedo (312bis, 312IS, seaplanes), (313) bomber/torpedo bomber, (314) coastal patrol torpedo bomber, (316) catapult reconnaissance seaplane.
Engines: (309) two 185hp Alfa Romeo A.115 six-in-line; (310, 316) two 470hp Piaggio P.VII C.16 seven-cylinder radials; (311, 312) two

continued ▶

Development: When the great Caproni combine took on Breda's designer Cesare Pallavicino it embarked on a series of modern aircraft of higher performance. The most important appeared to be the Ca 135 medium bomber, designed in the summer of 1934 to meet a Regia Aeronautica specification. A curious blend of wooden wings, light-alloy monocoque forward fuselage and steel tube plus fabric rear fuselage and tail, the prototype had two 800hp Isotta-Fraschini Asso engines but no guns. After over a year of testing the government ordered 14 as the Tipo Spagna to serve in the Spanish civil war. Peru bought six Tipo Peru, eventually purchasing 32. Yet the Ca 135 was not as good as the S.M.79 and Z.1007 by rival makers and the Regia Aeronautica kept delaying a decision. More powerful Fiat A.80 RC41 radials improved behaviour but at the expense of reliability and a good 135 did not appear until the Milan Aero Show in October 1937, when the Piaggio-engined 135bis was displayed. Though never adopted by the Regia Aeronautica it was frequently identified as having been used against Malta, Jugoslavia and Greece! The real raiders in these cases were probably BR.20s, but the 135 bis did find a customer: the Hungarian Air Force. Several hundred were operated by that service whilst attached to Luftflotte IV in the campaign on the Eastern Front in 1941—43.

Left: One of the colourful Ca 135bis bombers operated on the Eastern Front by the Hungarian Air Force (note tactical theatre marking of yellow bands). This example belonged to 4/III Bomb Group, but few of the Capronis lasted even until the end of 1942, and they were progressively replaced by superior German aircraft such as the Ju 88.

Above: The Ca 310 Libeccio was the first of the family to have retractable landing gear. This example is a civil-registered aircraft, probably used as a six-seat colonial transport, but most had a bomb-aimer's position in the nose and three machine guns, two fixed in the wing roots and one in the retractable turret.

Left: This Ca 310 is one of the armed multi-role models, and it was one of a batch sold in 1939 to the Norwegian army flying service (Haerens Flyvevàben). It was based at Sola airfield, Stavanger, where it was probably knocked out on 9 April 1940. The Ca 310 lacked the range to escape to Britain.

The Ca 314 was one of the most powerful and most important of the entire family. The fully glazed interior was similar to that of the Anson, but the Italian machine was much more powerful and this version could carry a torpedo.

650hp Piaggio P.XVI RC35 nine-cylinder radials; (313, 314) two 650hp Isotta-Fraschini Delta RC35 inverted-vee-12.

Dimensions: Span (309-312) 53ft 1¾in (16·20m), (313) 52ft 10½in (16·11m), (314) 54ft 7½in (16·65m), (316) 52ft 2in (15·90m); length (309) 43ft 7½in (13·30m), (311, 313, 314) 38ft 8in (11·79m), (310, 312) 40ft 0½in (12·20m), (316) 42ft 3in (12·88m); height 10ft 8in to 13ft 3in (floatplanes about 16ft 9in) (3·26 to 4·04m, floatplanes 5·10m).

Weights: Empty (309) 3,850lb (1746kg), (others) about 7,050lb (3200kg); loaded (309) 6,067lb (2750kg), (others) 10,252–13,580lb (4650–6160kg).

Performance: Maximum speed (309) 158mph (254km/h), (others) 227–271mph (365–435km/h) except 316 only 204mph (328km/h).

Armament: See text.

History: First flight (309) 1936; main production 1938–42.

Users: Italy (civil, RA, CB, ARSI, post-war AF), Germany (Luftwaffe), Croatia, Hungary, Jugoslavia, Norway, Spain, Sweden.

Development: This diverse family had wooden wings, and fuselages of welded steel tube covered with fabric. The Ghibli was a light multi-role machine for African use, with radio, cameras, light bomb racks and two machine guns (one fixed, one in a dorsal position). The more powerful examples carried up to five 12·7mm and three 7·7mm guns with bomb/torpedo loads up to 1,764lb (800kg). Total production of all models was about 2,400.

Below: The Ca 311 and (shown here) 312 had a streamlined nose with no stepped windscreen. The radial engines were similar in power to the aircooled inverted V-12s of the Ca 314 above.

Consolidated Vultee Model 32 B-24 Liberator

For variants, see text
(data for B-24J Liberator B.VI)

Origin: Consolidated Vultee Aircraft Corporation; also built by Douglas, Ford and North American Aviation.
Type: Long-range bomber with normal crew of ten.
Engines: Four 1,200hp Pratt & Whitney R-1830-65 Twin Wasp 14-cylinder two-row radials.
Dimensions: Span 110ft 0in (33·5m); length 67ft 2in (20·47m); height 18ft 0in (5·49m).
Weights: Empty 37,000lb (16,783kg); loaded 65,000lb (29,484kg).
Performance: Maximum speed 290mph (467km/h); initial climb 900ft (274m)/min; service ceiling 28,000ft (8534m); range at 190mph (306km/h) with 5,000lb (2268kg) bomb load 2,200 miles (3540km).
Armament: Ten 0·50in Brownings arranged in four electrically operated turrets (Consolidated or Emerson in nose, Martin dorsal, Briggs-Sperry retractable ventral "ball" and Consolidated or Motor Products tail) with two guns each plus two singles in manual waist positions; two bomb bays with roll-up doors with vertical racks on each side of central catwalk for up to 8,000lb (3629kg); two 4,000lb (1814kg) bombs could be hung externally on inner-wing racks instead of internal load.
History: First flight (XB-24) 29 December 1939; first delivery (LB-30A) March 1941; first combat service (Liberator I) June 1941; first combat service with US Army (B-24C) November 1941; termination of production 31 May 1945; withdrawal from service (various smaller air forces) 1955—56.
Users: Australia, Brazil, Canada, China, Czechoslovakia, France, India, Italy (CB), New Zealand, Portugal, South Africa, Soviet Union, Turkey, UK (RAF, BOAC), US (AAF, Navy, Marines); other countries post-war.

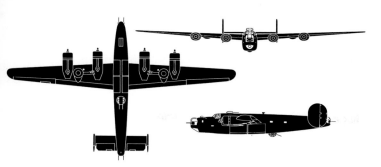

Above; Three-view of B-24H (B-24J similar except front turret).

Development: This distinctive aircraft was one of the most important in the history of aviation. Conceived five years after the B-17 it did not, in fact, notably improve on the older bomber's performance and in respect of engine-out performance and general stability and control it was inferior, being a handful for the average pilot. It was also by far the most complicated and expensive combat aircraft the world had seen — though in this it merely showed the way things were going to be in future. Yet it was built in bigger numbers than any other American aircraft in history, in more versions for more purposes than any other aircraft in history, and served on every front in World War II and with 15 Allied nations. In terms of industrial effort it transcended anything seen previously in any sphere of endeavour.

It had a curious layout, dictated by the slender Davis wing placed above the tall bomb bays. This wing was efficient in cruising flight, which combined with great fuel capacity to give the "Lib" longer range than any other landplane of its day. But it meant that the main gears were long, and they were retracted outwards by electric motors, nearly everything on board being electric. Early versions supplied to the RAF were judged not combat-ready, and they began the Atlantic Return Ferry Service as LB-30A transports. Better defences led to the RAF Liberator I, used by Coastal Command with ▶

Left: Though the B-17 Fortress was the more important USAAF bomber in the European theatre, the B-24 was made in much greater numbers and saw action on every Allied front, and with many air forces. This Liberator B.VI operated with 356 Sqn RAF from Salbani, India.

Below: One of the dramatic pictures taken on the raid on the Ploesti (Romania) refinery on 31 May 1944.

ASV radar and a battery of fixed 20mm cannon. The RAF Liberator II (B-24C) introduced power turrets and served as a bomber in the Middle East. The first mass-produced version was the B-24D, with turbocharged engines in oval cowls, more fuel and armament and many detail changes; 2,738 served US Bomb Groups in Europe and the Pacific, and RAF Coastal Command closed the mid-Atlantic gap, previously beyond aircraft range, where U-boat packs lurked.

Biggest production of all centred on the B-24G, H and J (Navy PB4Y and RAF B.VI and GR.VI), of which 10,208 were built. These all had four turrets, and were made by Convair, North American, Ford and Douglas. Other variants included the L and M with different tail turrets, the N with single fin, the luridly painted CB-24 lead ships, the TB-24 trainer, F-7 photo-reconnaissance, C-109 fuel tanker and QB-24 drone. There was also a complete family of Liberator Transport versions, known as C-87 Liberator Express to the Army, RY-3 to the Navy and C.VII and C.IX to the RAF, many having the huge single fin also seen on the PB4Y-2 Privateer. Excluding one-offs such as the redesigned R2Y transport and 1,800 equivalent aircraft delivered as spares, total production of all versions was a staggering 19,203. Their achievements were in proportion.

Consolidated Vultee Model 33 B-32 Dominator
XB-32, B-32 and TB-32

Origin: Consolidated Vultee Aircraft Corporation (Convair), Fort Worth, Texas; second-source production by Convair, San Diego.
Type: Long-range strategic bomber; (TB) crew trainer.
Engines: Four 2,300hp Wright R-3350-23 Duplex Cyclone 18-cylinder radials.
Dimensions: Span 135ft 0in (41·15m); length 83ft 1in (25·33m); height 32ft 9in (9·98m).
Weights: Empty 60,272lb (27,340kg); loaded 111,500lb (50,576kg); maximum 120,000lb (54,432kg).
Performance: Maximum speed 365mph (587km/h); service ceiling at normal loaded weight 35,000ft (10,670m); range (max bomb load) 800 miles (1287km), (max fuel) 3,800 miles (6115km).
Armament: (XB) two 20mm and 14 0·50in guns in seven remote-controlled turrets; (B) ten 0·50in in nose, two dorsal, ventral and tail turrets; max bomb load 20,000lb (9072kg) in tandem fuselage bays.
History: First flight (XB) 7 September 1942; service delivery (B) 1 November 1944.
User: USA (AAF).

Development: Ordered in September 1940, a month after the XB-29, the XB-32 was designed to the same Hemisphere Defense Weapon specification and followed similar advanced principles with pressurized cabins and remote-controlled turrets. Obviously related to the smaller B-24, the XB-32 had a slender wing passing above the capacious bomb bays, but the twin-wheel main gears folded into the large inner nacelles. There was a smoothly streamlined nose, like the XB-29, and twin fins. The second aircraft introduced a stepped pilot windscreen and the third a vast single fin like the final B-24 versions. Eventually the heavy and complex armament system was scrapped and replaced by simpler manned turrets, while in late 1943 the decision was taken to eliminate the troublesome pressurization and operate at 30,000ft or below. The B-32 was late and disappointing, though still a great performer. Large orders were placed at Fort Worth and

Above: To assist the gigantic formations of the 8th Air Force to form up, each Bomb Group had a distinctively painted lead ship. This spotted B-24H belonged to the 458th BG, based at Horsham St Faith, Norwich.

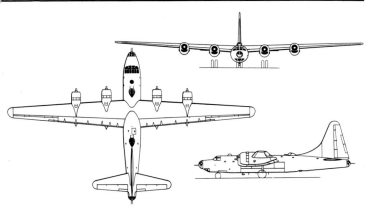

Above: Three-view of B-32 (TB-32 similar).

San Diego, but only 115 had been delivered by VJ-day and a single squadron in the Marianas made two combat missions.

Below: One of the production B-32 Dominators, with full armament. Few of these bombers saw active service.

Dornier Do 17

Do 17E, F, P, U and Z and Do 215

Origin: Dornier-Werke GmbH.
Type: (E, F, P) three-seat bomber (F = recon); (U) five-seat pathfinder; (Z, 215) four-seat bomber/recon.
Engines: (E, F) two 750hp BMW VI 7, 3 water-cooled vee-12; (P) two 865hp BMW 132N nine-cylinder radials; (Do 215B-1) two 1,075hp Daimler-Benz DB 601A 12-cylinder inverted-vee liquid-cooled.
Dimensions: (Both) span 59ft 0½in (18m); length 51ft 9½in (15·79m); height 14ft 11½in (4·56m).
Weights: Empty (Do 17Z-2) 11,484lb (5210kg); (Do 215B-1) 12,730lb (5775kg); loaded (both) 19,841lb (9000kg).
Performance: Maximum speed (Do 17Z-2) 263mph (425km/h); (Do 215B-1) 280mph (450km/h); service ceiling (Do 17Z-2) 26,740ft (8150m); (Do 215B-1) 31,170ft (9500m); range with half bomb load (Do 17Z-2) 721 miles (1160km); (Do 215B-1) 932 miles (1500km).
Armament: Normally six 7·92mm Rheinmetall MG 15 machine guns, one fixed in nose, remainder on manually aimed mounts in front windscreen, two beam windows, and above and below at rear; internal bomb load up to 2205lb (1000kg).
History: First flight (civil prototype) 23 November 1934; (Do 17Z-2) early 1939; (Do 215V1 prototype) late 1938; first delivery (Do 17Z-1) January 1939, (Do 215A-1) December 1939; termination of production (Do 17Z series) July 1940, (Do 215 series) January 1941.
Users: Croatia (puppet of Germany), Finland, Germany (Luftwaffe), Jugoslavia and Spain.

Development: Dornier designed the Do 17 as a fast passenger airliner, but made it so slim (early models got the nickname "Flying Pencil") that Lufthansa deemed it unacceptable for fare-paying customers. By chance ▶

Below: It is easy to see from this photograph why early versions of the Do 17 were called 'flying pencils'. This is a Do 17P-1, resembling the E and F (drawings, upper right) but with 865hp BMW 132N radials. It equipped 22 reconnaissance squadrons in 1939.

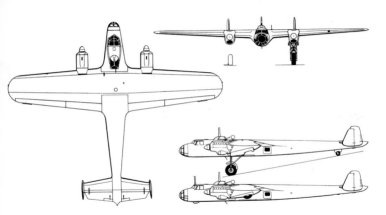

Above: Three-view of the first major Luftwaffe versions, the Do 17F-1 (reconnaissance) and (bottom) Do 17E-1 bomber.

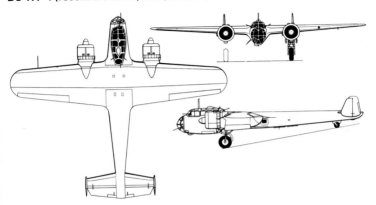

Above: Three-view of the Do 17Z-2.

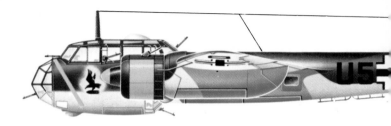

an Air Ministry officer test-flew a prototype and was so impressed he suggested it could form the basis of a bomber. By the end of 1935 the Do 17E and F were on order from three large factories, and with the more powerful P formed the basis of tactical bomber strength in the late 1930s. In 1938 Dornier produced a new and much more capacious nose housing four men and with a gun firing below to the rear. This led to the main wartime model, the Z, and 215.

Considerably heavier, the Do 17Z, powered by the Bramo radial, was at first underpowered and full bomb load had to await the more powerful Fafnir 323P of the 17Z-2. Between late 1939 and the summer of 1940 about 535 Do 17Z series bomber and reconnaissance machines were delivered and, though they suffered high attrition over Britain, they did much

Left: Most important of all Do 17 and 215 variants was the Do 17Z-2, the more powerful version of the new 1939 series with enlarged crew compartment rather like that of the larger and more capable Ju 88. This Z-2 belonged to III/KG 2, one of the crack Luftwaffe bomber units in the first two years of war. By the end of 1941 KG 2 had re-equipped with the Do 217E.

effective work and were the most popular and reliable of all Luftwaffe bombers of the early Blitzkrieg period. The Do 215 was the Do 17Z re-numbered as an export version, with the more powerful DB 601 engine. The Do 215A-1 for Sweden became the Do 215B-0 and B-1 for the Luftwaffe and altogether 101 were put into service for bomber and reconnaissance roles; 12 were converted as Do 215B-5 night intruders, with a "solid" nose carrying two cannon and four machine guns, and operated by night over Britain before transfer to Sicily in October 1941.

Below: Pumping hot air into a Do 17Z-2 of III/KG 3 in bitter weather on the Eastern Front about six months after the invasion of the Soviet Union. All were replaced by the end of 1942.

Dornier Do 217

Do 217E-2, K-2, M-1, J-2/N-2, P-1

Origin: Dornier-Werke GmbH.
Type: (E, K, M) four-seat bomber; (J, N) three-seat night fighter; (P) four-seat high-altitude reconnaissance.
Engines: (E-2, J-2) two 1,580hp BMW 801A or 801M 18-cylinder two-row radials; (K-2) two 1,700hp BMW 801D; (M-1, N-2) two 1,750hp Daimler-Benz DB 603A 12-cylinder inverted-vee liquid-cooled; (P-1) two 1,860hp DB 603B supercharged by DB 605T in the fuselage.
Dimensions: Span 62ft 4in (19m); (K-2) 81ft 4½in (24·8m); (P-1) 80ft 4in (24·4m); length 56ft 9¼in (17·3m); (E-2 with early dive brakes) 60ft 10½in (18·5m); (K-2 and M-1) 55ft 9in (17m); (J and N) 58ft 9in (17·9); (P) 58ft 11in (17·95m); height 16ft 5in (5m) (all versions same within 2in).
Weights: Empty (E-2) 19,522lb (8850kg); (M-1) 19,985 (9000kg); (K-2, J and N) all about 21,000lb (9450kg); (P) about 23,000lb (10,350kg); loaded (E-2) 33,070lb (15,000kg); (K-2, M-1) 36,817lb (16,570kg); (J and N) 30,203lb (13,590kg); (P) 35,200lb (15,840kg).
Performance: Maximum speed (E-2) 320mph (515km/h); (K-2) 333mph (533km/h); (M-1) 348mph (557km/h); (J and N) about 311mph (498km/h); (P) 488mph (781km/h); service ceiling (E-2) 24,610ft (7500m); (K-2) 29,530ft (9000m); (M-1) 24,140ft (7358m); (J and N) 27,560ft (8400m); (P) 53,000ft (16,154m); range with full bomb load, about 1,300 miles (2100km) for all versions.

Right: This Do 217E-2 R19 served with 9/KG 2 based at Gilze-Rijen on night missions against England in 1941-43. The designation suffix R19 denoted the fitting of MG 81Z, twin MG 81 guns in the tailcone.

Right: A Do 217E-5 of 6/KG 100 based at Istres, near Marseilles. This was one of the first aircraft to use the Hs 293 radio-guided missile in action.

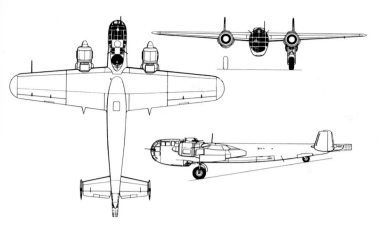

Above: The Do 217K-1 with new cockpit but original wing.

Armament: (E-2) one fixed 15mm MG 151/15 in nose, one 13mm MG 131 in dorsal turret, one MG 131 manually aimed at lower rear, and three 7·92mm MG 15 manually aimed in nose and beam windows; maximum bomb load 8818lb (4000kg), including 3307lb (1500kg) external; (K-2) defensive armament similar to E-2, plus battery of four 7·92mm MG 81 fixed rearward-firing in tail and optional pair fixed rearward-firing in nacelles (all sighted and fired by pilot), and offensive load of two FX 1400 ▶

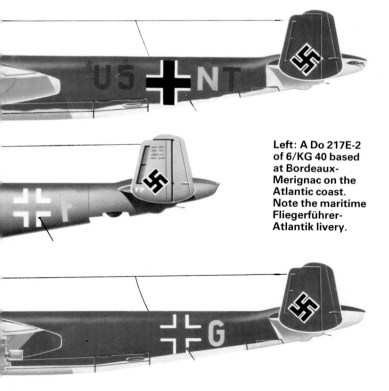

Left: A Do 217E-2 of 6/KG 40 based at Bordeaux-Merignac on the Atlantic coast. Note the maritime Fliegerführer-Atlantik livery.

radio-controlled glide bombs and/or (K-3 version) two Hs 293 air-to-surface rocket guided missiles; (M-1) as E-2 except MG 15s replaced by larger number of MG 81; (J-2 and N-2) typically four 20mm MG FF cannon and four 7·92mm MG 17 in nose plus MG 131 for lower rear defence (N-2 often had later guns such as MG 151/20 in nose and MG 151/20 or MK 108 30mm in Schräge Musik upward-firing installation); (P) three pairs of MG 81 for defence, and two 1102lb bombs on underwing racks.

History: First flight (Do 217V1) August 1938; (pre-production Do 217A-0) October or November 1939; first delivery of E series, late 1940; termination of production, late 1943.

Users: Germany (Luftwaffe), (217 J) Italy (RA).

Development: Superficially a scaled-up Do 215, powered at first by the same DB 601 engines, the 217 was actually considerably larger and totally different in detail design. Much of Dornier's efforts in 1938–40 were devoted to finding more powerful engines and improving the flying qualities, and when the BMW 801 radial was available the 217 really got into its stride and carried a heavier bomb load than any other Luftwaffe bomber of the time. Early E models, used from late 1940, had no dorsal turret and featured a

Above: Heaviest of all the regular Do 217 bomber versions was the 217K-2. Major structural stiffening and other changes allowed the wing span to be extended to 81ft 4½in and enabled takeoffs to be made with additional fuel as well as two of the monster Fritz-X radio-controlled bombs which weighed 3,454lb each. This aircraft, Werk-Nr 4572, was the first of the K-2 series.

very long extension of the rear fuselage which opened into an unusual dive brake. This was soon abandoned, but the 217 blossomed out into a prolific family which soon included the 217J night fighter, often produced by converting E-type bombers, and the N which was likewise produced by converting the liquid-cooled M. Several series carried large air-to-surface missiles steered by radio command from a special crew station in the bomber. Long-span K-2s of III/KG 100 scored many successes with their formidable missiles in the Mediterranean, their biggest bag being the Italian capital ship *Roma* as she steamed to the Allies after Italy's capitulation. The pressurised high-altitude P series had fantastic performance that would have put them out of reach of any Allied fighters had they been put into service in time. From 1943, Dornier devoted more effort to the technically difficult Do 317, which never went into service.

Left: In the foreground is a Do 217N-1 night fighter, with DB 603A liquid-cooled engines, FuG 202 Lichtenstein BC radar and heavy cannon armament. The subsequent N-2 version discarded the turret. In the background is an experimental prototype in the E-series.

Below: Still in factory code letters, this was the sixth of the pre-production batch of Do 217E-0 bombers of September/October 1940.

Douglas A-26 Invader

A-26 (later B-26) and JD-1 Invader; rebuilt as B-26K, redesignated A-26A

Origin: Douglas Aircraft Company; (post-war B-26K) On Mark Engineering.
Type: Three-seat attack bomber; FA-26 reconnaissance, JD target tug.
Engines: Two 2,000hp Pratt & Whitney R-2800-27, '-71 or -79 Double Wasp 18-cylinder two-row radials; On Mark B-26K, 2,500hp R-2800-103W.
Dimensions: Span 70ft (21·34m) (B-26K, 75ft, 22·86m, over tip tanks); length 50ft (15·24m); height 18ft 6in (5·64m).
Weights: Empty, typically 22,370lb (10,145kg); loaded, originally 27,000lb (12,247kg) with 32,000lb (14,515kg) maximum overload, later increased to 35,000lb (15,876kg) with 38,500lb (17,460kg) maximum overload.
Performance: Maximum speed 355mph (571km/h); initial climb 2,000ft (610m)/min; service ceiling 22,100ft (6736m); range with maximum bomb load 1,400 miles (2253km).
Armament: (A-26B) ten 0·5in Brownings, six fixed in nose and two each in dorsal and ventral turrets; internal bomb load of 4,000lb (1814kg), later supplemented by underwing load of up to 2,000lb (907kg); (A-26C) similar but only two 0·5in in nose; (B-26K, A-26A) various nose configurations with up to eight 0·5in or four 20mm, plus six 0·30in guns in wings and total ordnance load of 8,000lb (3629kg) in bomb bay and on eight outerwing pylons.
History: First flight (XA-26) 10 July 1942; service delivery December 1943; final delivery 2 January 1946; first flight of B-26K, February 1963.
Users: US (AAF, Navy).

Development: The Douglas Invader has a unique history. It was one of very few aircraft to be entirely conceived, designed, developed, produced in quantity and used in large numbers all during World War II. The whole programme was terminated after VJ-Day and anyone might have judged the aircraft finished. With new jets under development, Douglas made no effort to retain any design team on Invader development, neither did the Army Air Force show any interest. Yet this aircraft proved to be of vital importance in the Korean war and again in Vietnam and, by 1963, was urgently being manufactured for arduous front-line service. Some were in combat units 33 years after they were first delivered, a record no other kind of aircraft can equal. The design was prepared by Ed Heinemann at El Segundo as a natural successor to the DB-7 family, using the powerful new R-2800 engine. The Army Air Corps ordered three prototypes in May 1941, one with 75mm gun, one with four 20mm forward-firing cannon

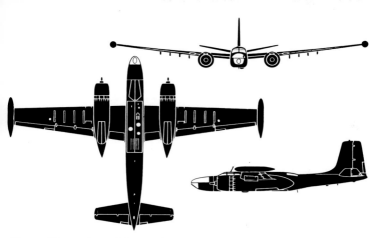

Above: Three-view of the much later B-26K.

and four 0·5in guns in an upper turret, with radar nose, and the third as an attack bomber with optical sighting station in the nose and two defensive turrets. In the event it was the bomber that was bought first, designated A-26B. Much faster than other tactical bombers with the exception of the Mosquito, it was 700lb lighter than estimate, and capable of carrying twice the specified bomb load. It was the first bomber to use a NACA laminar-flow airfoil, double-slotted flaps and remote-control turrets (also a feature of the B-29). Combat missions with the 9th AF began on 19 November 1944 and these aircraft dropped over 18,000 tons of bombs on European targets. A total of 1,355 A-26Bs were delivered, the last 535 having -79 engines boosted by water injection. The A-26C, in service in January 1945, had a transparent nose, lead-ship navigational equipment and was often fitted with H_2S panoramic radar; production of this model was 1,091. In 1948 the B-26 Marauder was retired from service and the Invaders were redesignated B-26. Over 450 were used in Korea, and in Vietnam these fine aircraft were one of the most favoured platforms for night attack on the Ho Chi Minh trail and in other interdiction areas. Though top speed was depressed to about 350mph, the A-26A (as the rebuilt B-26K was called) could carry up to 11,000lb (4990kg) of armament and deliver it accurately and, with 2 hr over target, over a wide radius. In 1977 six air forces retained Invader squadrons.

Below: Most of the Invaders used in World War II were 'solid-nosed' A-26bs. All ten heavy machine guns could fire ahead.

Douglas DB-7 family
A-20, Boston, Havoc

A-20, Boston, Havoc, BD-2, F-3 and P-70

Origin: Douglas Aircraft Company; (Boston IIIA, Boeing Airplane Company).

Type: Two-seat fighter and intruder, three-seat bomber or two-seat reconnaissance aircraft.

Engines: Early DB-7 versions (Boston I, II, Havoc II) two 1,200hp Pratt & Whitney R-1830-S3C4-G Twin Wasp 14-cylinder two-row radials; all later versions, two 1,500, 1,600 or 1,700hp Wright GR-2600-A5B, -11, -23 or -29 Double Cyclone 14-cylinder two-row radials.

Dimensions: Span 61ft 4in (18·69m); length varied from 45ft 11in to 48ft 10in (A-20G, 48ft 4in, 14·74m); height 17ft 7in (5·36m).

Weights: Early Boston/Havoc, typically empty 11,400lb (5171kg), loaded 16,700lb (7574kg); (A-20G, typical of main production) empty 12,950lb (5874kg), loaded 27,200lb (12,340kg).

Performance: Maximum speed, slowest early versions 295mph (475km/h); fastest versions 351mph (565km/h); (A-20G) 342mph (549km/h); initial climb 1,200–2,000ft (366–610m)/min; service ceiling typically 25,300ft (7720m); range with maximum weapon load typically 1,000 miles (1,610km).

Armament: (Havoc I), eight 0·303in Brownings in nose, one 0·303in Vickers K manually aimed in rear cockpit; (Havoc II) twelve 0·303in in nose, (Havoc intruder), four 0·303in in nose, one Vickers K, and 1,000lb (454kg) bomb load; (A-20B) two fixed 0·5in Brownings on sides of nose, one 0·5in manually aimed dorsal, one 0·30in manually aimed ventral, 2,000lb (907kg) bomb load; (Boston III bomber) four fixed 0·303in on sides of nose, twin manually aimed 0·303in dorsal, twin manually aimed 0·303in ventral, 2,000lb (907kg) bomb load; (Boston III intruder) belly tray of four 20mm Hispano cannon, 2,000lb (907kg) bomb load; (A-20G) four 20mm and two 0·5in or six 0·5in in nose, dorsal turret with two 0·5in, manually aimed 0·5in ventral, 4,000lb (1814kg) bomb load. Many other schemes, early A-20s having fixed rearward firing 0·30in in each nacelle.

History: First flight (Douglas 7B) 26 October 1938; (production DB-7) 17 August 1939; service delivery (France) 2 January 1940; termination of production September 1944.

Users: Australia, Brazil, Canada, France, Netherlands, New Zealand, South Africa, Soviet Union, UK (RAF), US (AAC/AAF, Navy).

Development: Designed by Jack Northrop and Ed Heinemann, the DB-7 family was one of the great combat aircraft of all time. Originally planned to meet a US Army Air Corps attack specification of 1938, it was dramatically altered and given more powerful Twin Wasp engines and a nosewheel-type landing gear (for the first time in a military aircraft). In February 1939 the French government ordered 100 of a further modified type, with deeper but narrower fuselage and other gross changes. This model, the DB-7, went into production at El Segundo and Santa Monica,

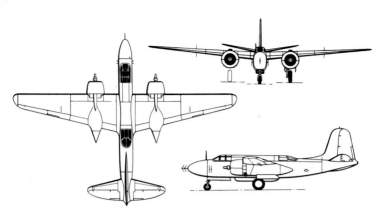

Above: Three-view of P-70 with four M-2 cannon and AI.IV radar.

with 1,764lb (800kg) bomb load and armament of six 7·5mm MAC 1934 machine guns. Delivery took place via Casablanca and about 100 reached the Armée de l'Air, beginning operations on 31 May 1940. Much faster than other bombers, the DB-7 was judged "hot", because it was a modern aircraft in an environment of small unpaved airfields and because it was very different, and more complex, than contemporary European machines. One unusual feature was the emergency control column in the rear gunner's cockpit for use if the pilot should be killed. A few DB-7s escaped to Britain, where most of the French order was diverted (increased to 270 by 1940), and over 100 were converted at Burtonwood, Lancs, into Havoc night fighters. Many Havocs had 2,700-million candlepower "Turbinlites" in the nose for finding enemy raiders by night, while 93 Sqn towed Long Aerial Mine charges on steel cables. In February 1942 the RAF began operations with the much more powerful Boston III; making daring daylight low-level raids over Europe, while production of the first US Army A-20s got into its stride. By far the most important model was the A-20G, with heavier bomb load, dorsal turret and devastating nose armament. Among many other important US Army versions were the P-70 night fighters and the transparent-nosed A-20J and K, often used as bombing lead ships by the 9th and 15th Air Forces (respectively in Northwest Europe and Italy). The RAF counterparts of the J and K were the Boston IV and V, of the 2nd Tactical Air Force and Desert AF (Italy). Total production of this hard-hitting aircraft was 7,385, of which 3,125 were supplied freely to the Soviet Union.

Left: Distinguished by its narrow, pointed vertical tail, this Havoc I was one of the first versions used by the RAF in 1940. A night intruder, in this case operated by 23 Sqn at Ford, Sussex, it retained a glazed nose; most later RAF Havocs were true night interceptors with a 'solid' nose filled with guns. The early Mk I had low-power Twin Wasp engines with locally added flame dampers, one of which is visible as a grey muff over the end of the exhaust pipe. Note old Vickers K rear gun.

Fairey Battle

Battle I to IV (data for II)

Origin: The Fairey Aviation Company; and Avions Fairey, Belgium; shadow production by Austin Motors.
Type: Three-seat light bomber.
Engine: One 1,030hp Rolls-Royce Merlin II vee-12 liquid-cooled.
Dimensions: Span 54ft 0in (16·46m); length 42ft 1¾in (12·85m); height 15ft 6in (4·72m).
Weights: Empty 6,647lb (3015kg); loaded 10,792lb (4895kg).
Performance: Maximum speed 241mph (388km/h); initial climb 920ft (280m)/min; service ceiling 25,000ft (7620m); range with bomb load at economical setting 900 miles (1448km).
Armament: One 0·303in Browning fixed in right wing and one 0·303in Vickers K manually aimed in rear cockpit; bomb load up to 1,000lb (454kg) in four cells in inner wings.
History: First flight (prototype) 10 March 1936; production Mk I, June 1937; final delivery January 1941; withdrawal from service 1949.
User: Australia, Belgium, Canada, Poland, South Africa, Southern Rhodesia, Turkey, UK (RAF).

Development: The Battle will forever be remembered as a combat aeroplane which seemed marvellous when it appeared and yet which, within four years, was being hacked out of the sky in droves so that, ever afterward, aircrew think of the name with a shudder. There was nothing faulty about the aircraft; it was simply a sitting duck for modern fighters. Designed to Specification P.27/32 as a replacement for the biplane Hart and Hind, this clean cantilever stressed-skin monoplane epitomised modern design and carried twice the bomb load for twice the distance at 50 per cent higher speed. It was the first aircraft to go into production with the new Merlin engine, taking its mark number (I, II, III or IV) from that of the engine. Ordered in what were previously unheard-of quantities (155, then 500 and then 863 from a new Austin 'shadow factory'), production built up faster than for any other new British aircraft; 15 RAF bomber squadrons were equipped between May 1937 and May 1938. When World War II began, more than 1,000 were in service and others were exported to Poland, Turkey and Belgium (where 18 were built by Avions Fairey). On 2 September 1939 ten Battle squadrons flew to France as the major offensive element of the Advanced Air Striking Force. They were plunged into furious fighting from 10 May 1940 and suffered grievously. On the first day of the Blitzkrieg in the West two members of 12 Sqn won posthumous VCs and four days later, in an all-out attack on German pontoon bridges at Sedan, 71 Battles attacked and 31 returned. Within six months all Battles were being replaced in front-line units and the survivors of the 2,419 built were shipped to Canada or Australia as trainers (many with separate instructor/pupil cockpits) or used as target tugs or test beds.

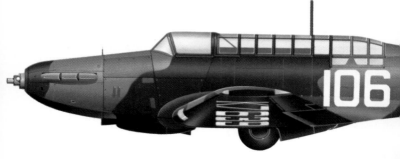

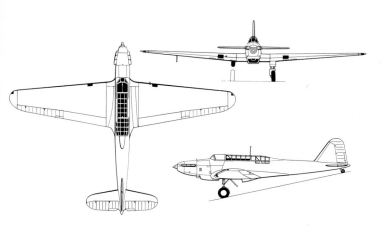

Above: Three-view of a standard Battle bomber (Mks I to IV).

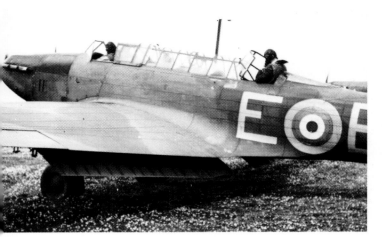

Above: Flap position suggests this Battle has just landed. The yellow roundel ring was added to most Battles after the débacle in France, where the usual roundel was equal radii red, white and blue, often with striped rudder (not fin).

Left: Battle I in 1938 markings serving with 106 Sqn. Officially called Type B, the two-colour roundels were similar to those used from World War I by heavy night bombers, and were adopted to render the Battles less conspicuous. But in 1940 white had been restored – not that it made much difference.

Farman F222

F 221, 222 and 223 series

Origin: SNCA du Centre (until 1936 the Farman company).
Type: All, basically, five-seat heavy bombers.
Engines: (F 221) four 800hp Gnome-Rhône GR14Kbrs 14-cylinder two-row radials; (F 222) four 860hp GR14Kbrs; (F 222/2) four 950hp GR14N 11/15 or Kirs; (F 223) four 1,100hp Hispano-Suiza HS14Aa08/09 vee-12 liquid-cooled; NC 223.3, four 910hp HS12Y29; (NC 223.4) four 1,050hp HS12Y37.
Dimensions: Span (F 221, 222, 222/2) 118ft 1$\frac{1}{2}$in (36m); (F 223, NC 223) 110ft 2$\frac{5}{8}$in (33·5m); length (F 221–222/2) 70ft 8$\frac{3}{4}$in (21·5m); (F 223, NC 223) 72ft 2in (22m); (NC 223.4) 77ft 1in (23·5m); height (all) 16ft 9in to 17ft 2$\frac{1}{4}$in (5·22m).
Weights: Empty (F 222/2) 23,122lb (10,488kg); (NC 223.3) 23,258lb (10,550kg); (NC 223.4) 22,046lb (10,000kg); loaded (F 221) 39,242lb (17,800kg); (F 222/2) 41,226lb (18,700kg); (NC 223.3) 42,329lb (19,200kg); (NC 223.4) 52,911lb (24,000kg).
Performance: Maximum speed (F 221) 185mph (300km/h); (F 222/2) 199mph (320km/h); (NC 223.3) 248mph (400km/h) (264mph as unarmed prototype); (NC 223.4) 239mph (385km/h); service ceiling (F 221) 19,700ft (6000m); (F 222/2) 26,250ft (8000m); (NC 223.3 at maximum weight) 24,606ft (7500m); (NC 223.4 at maximum weight) 13,120ft (4000m); range with maximum bomb load (F 221) 745 miles (1200km); F 222/2) 1,240 miles (2000km); (NC 223.3) 1,490 miles (2400km); (NC 223.4) 3,107 miles (5000km).
Armament: (F 221) three manually aimed 7·5mm MAC 1934 machine guns in nose turret, dorsal and ventral positions; bomb load seldom carried; (F 222/2) same guns as 221; normal bomb load of 5,510lb with maximum internal capacity of 9,240lb (4190kg); (NC 223·3) one MAC 1934 manually aimed in nose, one 20mm Hispano 404 cannon in SAMM 200 dorsal turret, one 20mm Hispano 404 in SAMM 109 ventral turret; internal bomb load of 9,240lb. NC 223·4, one manually aimed 7·5mm Darne machine gun in entry door; internal bomb load of 4,410lb (eight 250kg bombs).
History: First flight (F 211) October 1931; (F 221) 1933; (F 222) June

---

Fiat B.R. 20 Cicogna

B.R.20, 20M and 20 bis

Origin: Aeronautica d'Italia SA Fiat.
Type: Heavy bomber, with normal crew of five or six.
Engines: (B.R.20) two 1,000hp Fiat A.80 RC41 18-cylinder two-row radials; (B.R.20M) as B.R.20 or two 1,100hp A.80 RC20; (B.R.20bis) two 1,250hp A.82 RC32.
Dimensions: Span, 70ft 9in (21·56m); length, (B.R.20) 52ft 9in (16·2m);

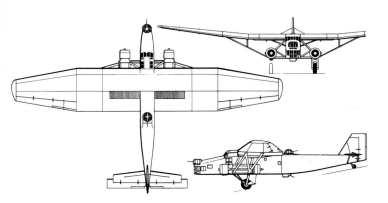

Above: Three-view of standard F 222/2.

1935; (F 222/2) October 1937; (NC 223) June 1937; (NC 223·3) October 1938; (NC 223·4) 15 March 1939.
User: France (Armée de l'Air, Aéronavale).

Development: This distinctive family formed the backbone of the Armée de l'Air heavy bomber force from 1935 until the collapse in 1940. It began with the F 210 of 1930, which set the pattern in having an angular box-like body, high-mounted wing and four engines slung on braced struts from the wing and fuselage in push/pull double nacelles. By way of the 220 came the 221, which served mainly as a 20-seat troop transport. The 222 introduced retractable landing gear, and the 36 F. 222/2 bombers of GBI/15 and II/15 served tirelessly in the dark months of 1940, often flying bombing missions by night over Germany and even Italy and as transports in North Africa until late 1944. The NC. 223.3, developed after nationalization, was a complete redesign and the most powerful and capable night bomber of 1938–40. The 223.4, a transatlantic mailplane, served with the Aéronavale as a heavy bomber, and in an epic 13hr 30min flight on 7–8 June 1940 one bombed Berlin.

(B.R.20M, 20bis) 55ft 0in (16·78m); height 15ft 7in (4·75m).
Weights: Empty (all), about 14,770lb (6700kg); loaded (B.R.20) 22,046lb (10,000kg); (B.R.20M) 23,038lb (10,450kg).
Performance: Maximum speed, (B.R.20) 264mph (425km/h); (B.R.20M) 267mph (430km/h); (B.R.20bis) 292mph (470km/h); initial climb (all) about 902ft (275m)/min; service ceiling, (B.R.20, 20M) 22,145ft (6750m); (B.R.20bis) 26,246ft (8000m); range, (B.R.20, 20M) 1,243 miles (2000km); (B.R.20bis) 1,710 miles (2750km).
Armament: (B.R.20) four 7·7mm Breda-SAFAT machine guns in nose turret (one), dorsal turret (two) and manual ventral position; bomb load 3,527lb (1600kg); (B.R.20M) as B.R.20 except nose gun 12·7mm; ▶

Left: One of the more uncommon Fiat B.R.20 Cicogna bombers was this example from a batch supplied to the Japanese Army in 1937. No fewer than 75 were delivered, seeing action in both the Chinese campaign and World War II. The aircraft illustrated served with the 1st Chutai, 12th Hikosentai. Japanese designation was Yi-shiki.

(B.R.20bis) as B.R.20M with two extra 12·7mm guns manually aimed from lateral blisters; bomb load 5,511lb (2500kg).

History: First flight (prototype) 10 February 1936; service delivery, September 1936; first flight (B.R.20M) late 1939; first flight B.R.20bis, December 1941.

Users: Hungary, Italy (RA), Japan, Spain, Venezuela.

Development: Ing Rosatelli was responsible for a great series of B.R. (Bombardamento Rosatelli) designs from 1919 onwards. Most were powerful single-engined biplanes, but in the mid-1930s he very quickly produced the B.R.20, a large monoplane with stressed-skin construction and other modern refinements. Despite its relative complexity the original aircraft was put into production within six months of the first flight and by the end of 1936 the B.R.20-equipped 13° Stormo was probably the most advanced bomber squadron in the world. Fiat also built two civil B.R.20L record-breakers, and also offered the new bomber for export, soon gaining a valuable order for 85, not from the expected China but from Japan, which needed a powerful bomber to bridge the gap caused by a delay with the Army Ki-21. In June 1937 the B.R.20 figured prominently in the Aviazione Legionaria sent to fight for the Nationalists in Spain and, with the He 111, bore the brunt of their very successful bomber operations. Spain purchased a manufacturing licence, which was not taken up, and purchased at least 25 from Fiat. An additional number were brought by Venezuela. In 1940, when Italy entered World War II, some 250 had been delivered to the Regia Aeronautica, the last 60 being of the strengthened and much more shapely M (Modificato) type. In October 1940 two groups of 37 and 38 of the M model operated against England, but they were hacked down with ease and were recalled in January 1941. During 1942 the B.R.20 began to fade, becoming used for ocean patrol, operational training and bombing where opposition was light. A large force supported the Luftwaffe in Russia, where casualties were heavy. By the Armistice only 81 of all versions were left out of 606 built. The much improved B.R.20bis never even got into bulk production.

Above: Late-production Fiat B.R.20M Cicognas of the 276th Squadriglia operating on the Eastern front in 1942. Even when assigned to relatively 'easy' sectors they suffered heavy losses.

Below: The blunter outline of the original production version can be seen in this action picture of B.R.20s of the Aviazione Legionaria operating in Spain in late 1937.

Focke-Wulf Fw 200 Condor

Fw 200C-0 to C-8

Origin: Focke-Wulf Flugzeugbau GmbH, in partnership with Hamburger Flugzeugbau (Blohm und Voss).

Type: Maritime reconnaissance bomber and (C-6 to -8) missile launcher, many used as transports.

Engines: Usually four 1,200hp BMW-Bramo Fafnir 323R-2 nine-cylinder radials.

Dimensions: Span 107ft 9½in (30·855m); length 76ft 11½in (23·46m); height 20ft 8in (6·3m).

Weights: (C-3/U-4) empty 28,550lb (12,951kg); loaded 50,045lb (22,700kg).

Performance: Maximum speed (C-3) 224mph (360km/h); (C-8) 205mph (330km/h); initial climb, about 656ft (200m)/min; service ceiling 19,030ft (5800m); range with standard fuel, 2,206 miles (3550km).

Armament: Typical C-3/C-8, one forward dorsal turret with one 15mm MG 151/15 (or 20mm MG 151/20 or one 7·92mm MG 15), one 20mm MG 151/20 manually aimed at front of ventral gondola, three 7·92mm MG 15 manually aimed at rear of ventral gondola and two beam windows (beam guns sometimes being 13mm MG 131) and one 13mm MG 131 in aft dorsal position; maximum bomb load of 4,626lb (2100kg) carried in gondola and beneath outer wings (C-6, C-8, two Hs 293 guided missiles carried under outboard nacelles).

History: First flight (civil prototype) 27 July 1937; (Fw 200C-0) January, 1940; final delivery (C-8) February 1944.

User: (Fw 200C series) Germany (Luftwaffe).

Development: Planned solely as a long-range commercial transport for the German airline Deutsche Luft Hansa, the prewar Fw·200 prototypes set up impressive record flights to New York and Tokyo and attracted export orders from Denmark, Brazil, Finland and Japan. Transport prototype and production versions were also used by Hitler and Himmler as VIP executive machines and several later variants were also converted as special transports. In 1938 the Japanese asked for one Condor converted for use as a long-range ocean reconnaissance machine. The resulting Fw 200V-10 prototype introduced a ventral gondola and led to the Fw 200C-0 as the prototype of a Luftwaffe aircraft which had never been requested or planned and yet which was to prove a most powerful instrument of war. Distinguished by long-chord cowlings, twin-wheel main gears (because of the increased gross weight) and a completely new armament and equipment fit, the C-0 led to the C-1, used operationally from June 1940 by KG 40 at Bordeaux-Mérignac. By September 1940 this unit alone had sunk over 90,000 tons of Allied shipping and for the next three years the C-series Condors were in Churchill's words, "the scourge of the Atlantic". But, though the Fw 200 family continued to grow in equipment

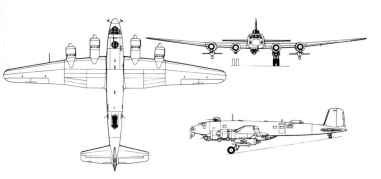

Above: The Fw 200C-8/U10, the final sub-type, with Hs 293s.

Below: One of the ultimate production variant, the Fw 200C-8, with FuG 200 Hohentwiel nose radar, HDL 151 cannon turret and racks for Hs 293 Missiles under and outboard of the engines.

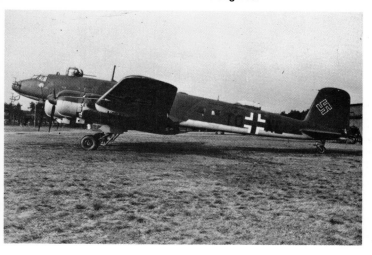

and lethality, the Allies fought back with long-range Coastal Command aircraft, escort carriers and CAM (Catapult-Armed Merchantman) fighters and by mid-1944 surviving Condors were being forced into transport roles on other fronts. Total production was 276 and one of the fundamental failings of the Condor was structural weakness, catastrophic wing and fuselage failures occurring not only in the air but even on the ground, on take-off or landing.

Left: Typical of the Condors that earned the apellation 'scourge of the Atlantic' in 1940–42, this Fw 200C-3 served with KG 40 at Cognac and Bordeaux-Merignac from early 1941. The front turret had only a 7·92mm gun but a 20mm cannon was in the front of the gondola and the hand-held rear guns were often all 13mm MG131s.

Fokker C.X

C.X

Origin: NV Fokker, Netherlands; licence built by Valtion Lentokonetehdas, Finland.
Type: Two-seat bomber and reconnaissance.
Engine: (Dutch) one 650hp Rolls-Royce Kestrel V vee-12 liquid-cooled; (Finnish) one licence-built 835hp Bristol Pegasus XXI nine-cylinder radial.
Dimensions: Span, 39ft 4in (12m); length (Kestrel) 30ft 2in (9·2m); (Pegasus) 29ft 9in (9·1m); height, 10ft 10in (3·3m).
Weights: Empty (both), about 3,086lb (1400kg); loaded (Kestrel) 4,960lb (2250kg); (Pegasus) 5,512lb (2500kg).
Performance: Maximum speed (Kestrel) 199mph (320km/h); (Pegasus) 211mph (340km/h); service ceiling (Kestrel) 27,230ft (8300m); (Pegasus) 27,560ft (8400m); range (Kestrel) 516 miles (830km), (Pegasus) 522 miles (840km).
Armament: Two 7·9mm machine guns fixed in top of front fuselage and third manually aimed from rear cockpit; underwing racks for two 385lb (175kg) or four 221lb (100kg) bombs.
History: First flight 1934; service delivery (Dutch) 1937; (Finnish) 1938.
Users: Finland, Netherlands.

Development: Derived from the C.V-E and planned as a successor, the C.X was a notably clean machine typical of good military design of the mid-1930s. By this time world-wide competition was very severe and Fokker could not achieve such widespread export success. The first orders were for ten for the Royal Netherlands East Indies Army, followed by 20 for the RNethAF (then called Luchtvaartafdeling, LVA), the last 15 having enclosed cockpits and tailwheels. Further small numbers were made in Holland, at least one having a 925hp Hispano-Suiza 12Y engine with 20mm cannon firing through the propeller hub. Fokker also developed a considerably more capable C.X for Finland, with the Pegasus radial. The Finnish State Aircraft Factory at Tampere went into licence-production with this version in 1938, the engine being made at Tammerfors. The Finnish C.X had an enclosed heated cockpit, rapid cold-weather starting and either wheel or ski landing gear. All available Dutch and Finnish C.X aircraft participated in World War II. None of the LVA machines survived the "Five Day War" of 10–15 May 1940, but the Finnish aircraft continued until at least 1944 under severe conditions and finally went into action not against the Russians but in helping them drive the Germans from Finnish territory in 1944–45.

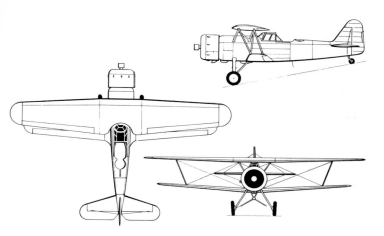

Above: Three-view of Finnish C.X with wheel landing gear.

Above: Though the pointed-nose Dutch C.X
with water-cooled Rolls-Royce Kestrel engine
saw brief action on 10 May 1940 the chief version
in World War II was this radial-engined Finnish
variant. The State Aircraft Factory at
Tammerfors delivered 30 by 1938, and then built
a further five in 1942 to replace combat losses.

Left: This illustration of one of the
special Pegasus-engined C.X bomber-
reconnaissance aircraft made under licence
in Finland shows the streamlined ski
landing gears used in winter. Though by
1939 it represented an outmoded type the
C.X was always popular with its crews.
Sadly, the last in active service was destroyed
in an accident in 1958.

Handley Page Halifax

H.P.57 Halifax I, H.P.59 Mk II Series 1A, III, H.P.61 Mk V, B.VI and VII, C.VIII and A.IX

Origin: Handley Page Ltd; also built by London Aircraft Production Group, English Electric Ltd, Rootes Securities (Speke) and Fairey Aviation Ltd (Stockport).

Type: Seven-seat heavy bomber; later ECM platform, special transport and glider tug, cargo transport and paratroop carrier.

Engines: Four Rolls-Royce Merlin vee-12 liquid-cooled or Bristol Hercules 14-cylinder two-row sleeve-valve radial (see text).

Dimensions: Span (I to early III) 98ft 10in (30·12m); (from later III) 104ft 2in (31·75m); length (I, II, III Srs 1) 70ft 1in (21·36m); (II Srs 1A onwards) 71ft 7in (21·82m); height 20ft 9in (6·32m).

Weights: Empty (I Srs 1) 33,860lb (15,359kg), (II Srs 1A) 35,270lb (16,000kg); (VI) 39,000lb (17,690kg); loaded (I) 55,000lb (24,948kg); (I Srs 1) 58,000lb (26,308kg); (I Srs 2) 60,000lb (27,216kg); (II) 60,000lb; (II Srs 1A) 63,000lb (28,576kg), (III) 65,000lb (29,484kg), (V) 60,000lb; (VI) 68,000lb (30,844kg); (VII, VIII, IX) 65,000lb.

Performance: Maximum speed (I) 265mph (426km/h); (II) 270mph (435km/h); (III, VI) 312mph (501km/h); (V, VII, VIII, IX) 285mph (460 km/h); initial climb (typical) 750ft (229m)/min; service ceiling, typically (Merlin) 22,800ft (6950m); (Hercules) 24,000ft (7315m); range with maximum load (I) 980 miles (1577km); (II) 1,100 miles (1770km); (III, VI) 1,260 miles (2030km).

Armament: See text.

History: First flight (prototype) 25 October 1939; (production Mk I) 11 October 1940; squadron delivery 23 November 1940; first flight (production III) July 1943; final delivery 20 November 1946.

Users: Australia, Canada, France (FFL), New Zealand, UK (RAF, BOAC).

Development: Though it never attained the limelight and glamour of its partner, the Lancaster, the "Halibag" made almost as great a contribution to Allied victory in World War II, and it did so in a far greater diversity of roles. Planned as a twin-Vulture bomber to Specification P.13/36 with a gross weight of 26,300lb it grew to weigh 68,000lb as a formidable weapon platform and transport that suffered from no vices once it had progressed through a succession of early changes. By far the biggest change, in the summer of 1937, was to switch from two Vultures to four Merlins (a godsend, as it turned out) and the first 100 H.P.57s were ordered on 3 September 1937. This version, the Mk I, had a 22ft bomb bay and six bomb cells in the wing centre-section. Engines were 1,280hp Merlin X and defensive armament comprised two 0·303in Brownings in the nose turret, four in the tail turret and, usually, two in manual beam positions. The first squadron was No 35 at Linton on Ouse and the first mission Le Havre on the night of 11/12 March 1942. The I Srs 2 was stressed to 60,000lb and the Srs 3 had more fuel. The Mk II had 1,390hp Merlin XX and Hudson-type twin-0·303in dorsal turret instead of beam guns. On the II Srs 1 Special the

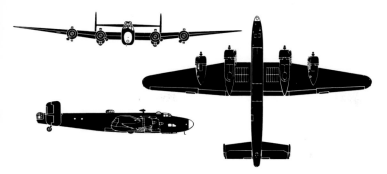

Above: Three-view of the extended-span Halifax B.111 Series II (Mk VI similar). Most had H$_2$S radar fitted.

Above: L9530 was one of the first production batch in 1940. Serving with 76 Sqn (MP-L) it had manual beam guns and prominent fuel-jettison pipes passing beneath the flaps. The photograph must have been taken from the right beam gun position of an accompanying Halifax, in mid-1941. The white object under the outer left wing is the landing light.

Left: A Halifax B.III Series II with extended wings and H$_2$S serving with 640 Sqn at Leconfield, Yorkshire. Vivid tails were common among the multi-national Halifax units which included important contributions from Canada and free France.

front and dorsal turrets and engine flame dampers were all removed to improve performance. The II Srs 1A introduced what became the standard nose, a clear Perspex moulding with manually aimed 0·303in Vickers K, as well as the Defiant-type 4×0·303in dorsal turret and 1,390hp Merlin XXII. Later Srs 1A introduced larger fins which improved bombing accuracy; one of these, with radome under the rear fuselage, was the first aircraft to use H_2S ground-mapping radar on active service. In November 1942 the GR.II Srs 1A entered service with Coastal Command, with 0·5in nose gun, marine equipment and often four-blade propellers. The III overcame all the performance problems with 1,650hp Hercules and DH Hydromatic propellers, later IIIs having the wings extended to rounded tips giving better field length, climb, ceiling and range. The IV (turbocharged Hercules) was not built. The V was a II Srs 2A with Dowty landing gear and hydraulics (Messier on other marks), used as a bomber, Coastal GR, ASW and meteorological aircraft. The VI was the definitive bomber, with 1,800hp Hercules 100 and extra tankage and full tropical equipment. The VII was a VI using old

Above: One of the first Halifax II Series 1 (the large number 9 is not explained) photographed on factory test in late 1941. Slowest of all marks, this had a Hudson-type dorsal turret instead of beam guns, plus flame-damped exhausts.

Hercules XVI. The C.VIII was an unarmed transport with large quick-change 8,000lb cargo pannier in place of the bomb bay and 11 passenger seats; it led to the post-war Halton civil transport. The A.IX carried 16 paratroops and associated cargo. The III, V, VII and IX served throughout Europe towing gliders and in other special operations, including airdropping agents and arms to Resistance groups and carrying electronic countermeasures (ECM) with 100 Group. Total production amounted to 6,176, by H.P., English Electric, the London Aircraft Production Group (London Transport), Fairey and Rootes, at a peak rate of one per hour. Final mission was by a GR.VI from Gibraltar in March 1952, the Armée de l'Air phasing out its B.VI at about the same time.

71

Handley Page Hampden

H.P.52 Hampden I and H.P.53 Hereford I

Origin: Handley Page Ltd; also built by English Electric Co. and Canadian Associated Aircraft.

Type: Four-seat bomber (Hampden, later torpedo bomber and minelayer).

Engines: (Hampden) two 1,000hp Bristol Pegasus XVIII nine-cylinder radials; (Hereford) two 1,000hp Napier Dagger VIII 24-cylinder H-type air-cooled.

Dimensions: Span 69ft 2in (21·98m); length 53ft 7in (16·33m); height 14ft 4in (4·37m).

Weights: Empty (Hampden) 11,780lb (5344kg); (Hereford) 11,700lb (5308kg); loaded (Hampden) 18,756lb (8508kg); (Hereford) 16,000lb (7257kg).

Performance: (Hampden) maximum speed 254mph (410km/h); initial climb 980ft (300m)/min; service ceiling 19,000ft (5790m); range with maximum bomb load 1,095 miles (1762km).

Armament: Originally, one offensive 0·303in Vickers fixed firing ahead, one 0·303in Lewis manually aimed from nose by nav/bomb aimer, one Lewis manually aimed by wireless operator from upper rear position and one Lewis manually aimed by lower rear gunner; bomb load of 4,000lb (1814kg). By January 1940 both rear positions had twin 0·303in Vickers K with increased field of fire. Hard points for two 500lb bombs added below outer wings, provision for carrying mines or one 18in torpedo internally.

History: First flight (H.P.52 prototype) 21 June 1936; (production Hampden I) May 1938; (Hereford I) December 1939; termination of production March 1942.

Users: Canada, New Zealand, UK (RAF).

Development: On paper the Hampden, the last of the monoplane bombers to enter RAF service during the Expansion Scheme of 1936—38, was a truly outstanding aircraft. The makers considered it so fast and manoeuvrable they called it "a fighting bomber" and gave the pilot a fixed gun. They judged the three movable guns gave complete all-round defence without the penalties of heavy turrets and, while the Hampden was almost the equal of the big Whitley and Wellington in range with heavy bomb load, it was much faster than either; it was almost as fast as the Blenheim, but carried four times the load twice as far (on only fractionally greater power). Thanks to its well flapped and slatted wing it could land as slowly as 73mph. Designed to B.9/32, the prototype was angular but the production machine, to 30/36, looked very attractive and large orders were placed, eight squadrons being operational at the start of World War II. Hampdens were busy in September 1939 raiding German naval installations and ships (bombing German land was forbidden), until the daylight formations encountered enemy fighters. Then casualties were so heavy the Hampden was taken off operations and re-equipped with much better armament and armour — and, ▶

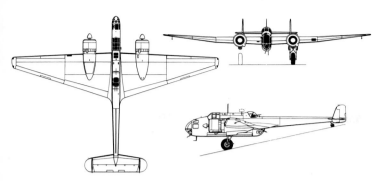

Above: Hampden I in 1940 with twin dorsal and ventral guns.

Above: This photograph taken from the upper rear gunner's position, probably in 1940, shows three other Hampdens in line astern. Though exceptionally manoeuvrable, the Hampden proved in practice to have no significant capability as a fighter, though the fixed nose gun was retained. More important was the decision, pushed by Guy Gibson, to fit twin guns at the rear.

Left: A Hampden I of No 44 (Rhodesia) Sqn, based at Waddington in 1940 and painted in that period's markings with black sides and with lettering in Dull Red. In June 1942 the white and yellow in the national insignia was made thinner (one-eighth of the total) to reduce contrast at night. By that time No 44 had become first squadron to convert to the Lancaster, a far more formidable aircraft.

73

more to the point, used only at night. Despite cramp and near-impossibility of getting from one crew position to another, the "Flying Suitcase" had a successful career bombing invasion barges in the summer of 1940, bombing German heartlands, mine-laying and, finally, as a long-range torpedo bomber over the North Sea and northern Russia. Handley Page built 500, English Electric built 770 and Canadian Associated Aircraft 160. Short Brothers built 100 Herefords which never became operational; many were converted to Hampdens.

Top: A Hampden I (there was only the one basic mark) of RAF No 455 Sqn, based at Leuchars in late 1941. The added external 500lb bomb rack under the right wing can be clearly seen.

Above: A fine portrait of Hampdens of No 44 (Rhodesia) Sqn, taken in early 1942. This was immediately before the squadron re-equipped with the Lancaster and became the envy of Bomber Command. Compare with the picture on pages 14–15.

Heinkel He 111

He 111 B series, E series, H series and P series

Origin: Ernst Heinkel AG; also built in France on German account by SNCASO; built under licence by Fabrica de Avione SET, Romania, and CASA, Spain.

Type: Four-seat or five-seat medium bomber (later, torpedo bomber, glider tug and missile launcher).

Engines: (He 111H-3) two 1,200hp Junkers Jumo 211D-2 12-cylinder inverted-vee liquid-cooled; (He 111P-2) two 1,100hp Daimler-Benz DB 601A-1 12-cylinder inverted-vee liquid-cooled.

Dimensions: (H-3) Span 74ft $1\frac{3}{4}$in (22·6m); length 53ft $9\frac{1}{2}$in (16·4m); height 13ft $1\frac{1}{2}$in (4m).

Weights: Empty (H-3) 17,000lb (7720kg); (P-2) 17,640lb (8000kg); maximum loaded (H-3) 30,865lb (14,000kg); (P-2) 29,762lb (13,500kg).

Performance: Maximum speed (H-3) 258mph (415km/h); (P-2) 242mph (390km/h) at 16,400ft (5000m) (at maximum weight, neither version could exceed 205mph, 330km/h); climb to 14,765ft (4500m) 30—35min at normal gross weight, 50min at maximum; service ceiling (both) around 25,590ft (7800m) at normal gross weight, under 16,400ft (5000m) at maximum; range with maximum bomb load (both) about 745 miles (1200km).

Armament: (P-2) 7·92mm Rheinmetall MG 15 machine gun on manual mountings in nosecap, open dorsal position and ventral gondola; (H-3) same, plus fixed forward-firing MG 15 or 17, two MG 15s in waist windows and

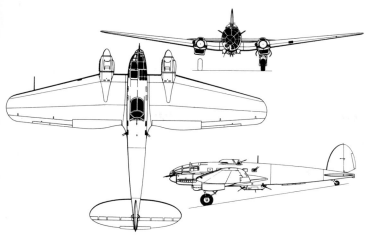

Above: A fairly late bomber variant, the He 111H-16.

(usually) 20mm MG FF cannon in front of ventral gondola and (sometimes) fixed rear-firing MG 17 in extreme tail; internal bomb load up to 4,410lb (2000kg) in vertical cells, stored nose-up; external bomb load (at expense of internal) one 4,410lb (2000kg) on H-3, one or two 1,102lb (500kg) on others; later marks carried one or two 1,686lb (765kg) torpedoes, Bv 246 glide missiles, Hs 293 rocket missiles, Fritz X radio-controlled glide bombs or one FZG-76 ("V-1") cruise missile. *continued* ▶

Left: The most numerous He 111 model was the H-6, which was often used with a 20mm MG FF firing forward from the gondola against ships. This H-6 served with II/KG 26 from Ottana, Sardinia, in 1943.

Below, left: An SC2000 bomb (4,410lb) about to be hung under a Heinkel of KG 26 on a mission over southern England in late 1940

Below: Bombs fell tail-first and tumbled wildly.

Above: He 111P-1 bombers photographed in spring 1939 serving with III/KG 255, which on 1 May 1939 was redesignated III/KG 51. Later the P-1 was supplanted by the Jumo-powered H-series.

Below: Armourers of KG 55 pulling an SC 500 bomb of 1,102lb on the Russian front soon after Operation Barbarossa in June 1941. The aircraft is an He 111H-6, the most numerous version.

History: First flight (He 111V1 prototype) 24 February 1935; (pre-production He 111B-0) August 1936; (production He 111B-1) 30 October 1936; (first He 111E series) January 1938; (first production He 111P-1) December 1938; (He 111H-1) January or February 1939; final delivery (He 111H-23) October 1944; (Spanish C.2111) late 1956.

Users: China, Germany (Luftwaffe, Luft Hansa), Hungary, Iraq, Romania, Spain, Turkey.

Development: A natural twin-engined outgrowth of the He 70, the first He 111 was a graceful machine with elliptical wings and tail, secretly flown as a bomber but revealed to the world a year later as a civil airliner. Powered by 660hp BMW VI engines, it had typical armament of three manually aimed machine guns but the useful bomb load of 2,200lb (1000kg) stowed nose-up in eight cells in the centre fuselage. In 1937 a number of generally similar machines secretly flew photo-reconnaissance missions over Britain, France and the Soviet Union, in the guise of airliners of Deutsche Luft Hansa. In the same year the He 111B-1 came into Luftwaffe service, with two 880hp Daimler-Benz DB 600C engines, while a vast new factory was built at Oranienburg solely to make later versions. In February 1937 operations began with the Legion Kondor in Spain, with considerable success, flight performance being improved in the B-2 by 950hp DB 600CG engines which were retained in the C series. The D was faster, with the 1,000hp Jumo 211A-1, also used in the He 111 F in which a new straight-edged wing was introduced. To a considerable degree the success of the early elliptical-winged He 111 bombers in Spain misled the Luftwaffe into considering that nothing could withstand the onslaught of their huge fleets of medium bombers. These aircraft — the trim Do 17, the broad-winged He 111 and the

Above: The pale theatre band ahead of the tail (yellow for the Eastern front, white for the Mediterranean) shows that this photo, taken from alongside the pilot, dates from later than 1940. The slow Heinkel never did find satisfactory defensive armament.

high-performance Ju 88 — were all extremely advanced by the standards of the mid-1930s when they were designed. They were faster than the single-seat fighters of that era and, so the argument went, therefore did not need much defensive armament. So the three machine guns carried by the first He 111 bombers in 1936 stayed unchanged until, in the Battle of Britain, the He 111 was hacked down with ease, its only defence being its toughness and ability to come back after being shot to pieces. The inevitable result was that more and more defensive guns were added, needing a fifth or even a sixth crew-member. Coupled with incessant growth in equipment and armour the result was deteriorating performance, so that the record-breaker of 1936—38 became the lumbering sitting duck of 1942—45. Yet the He 111 was built in ever-greater numbers, virtually all the later sub-types being members of the prolific H-series. Variations were legion, including versions with large barrage-balloon deflectors, several kinds of missiles (including a V-1 tucked under the left wing root), while a few were completed as saboteur transports. The most numerous version was the H-6, and the extraordinary He 111Z (Zwilling) glider tug of 1942 consisted of two H-6s joined by a common centre wing carrying a fifth engine. Right to the end of the war the RLM and German industry failed to find a replacement for the old "Spaten" (spade). and the total produced in Germany and Romania was at least 6,086 and possibly more than 7,000. Merlin-engined C.2111 versions continued in production in Spain until 1956.

Heinkel He 177 Greif

He 177A-0 to A-5, He 277 and He 274

Origin: Ernst Heinkel AG; also built by Arado Flugzeugwerke.

Type: He 177, six-seat heavy bomber and missile carrier.

Engines: Two 2,950hp Daimler-Benz DB 610A-1/B-1, each comprising two inverted-vee-12 liquid-cooled engines geared to one propeller.

Dimensions: Span 103ft 1¾in (31·44m); length 72ft 2in (22m); height 21ft (6·4m).

Weights: Empty 37,038lb (16,800kg); loaded (A-5) 68,343lb (31,000kg).

Performance: Maximum speed (at 41,000lb, 18,615kg) 295mph (472 km/h); initial climb 853ft (260m)/min; service ceiling 26,500ft (7080m); range with FX or Hs 293 missiles (no bombs) about 3,107 miles (5000km).

Armament: (A-5/R2) one 7·92mm MG 81J manually aimed in nose, one 20mm MG 151 manually aimed at front of ventral gondola, one or two 13mm MG 131 in forward dorsal turret, one MG 131 in rear dorsal turret, one MG 151 manually aimed in tail and two MG 81 or one MG 131 manually aimed at rear of gondola; maximum internal bomb load 13,200lb (6000kg), seldom carried; external load, two Hs 293 guided missiles, FX 1400 guided bombs, mines or torpedoes (more if internal bay blanked off and racks added below it).

History: First flight (He 177V-1) 19 November 1939; (pre-production He 177A-0) November 1941; service delivery (A-1) March 1942; (A-5) February 1943; first flight (He 277V-1) December 1943; (He 274, alias AAS 01A) December 1945.

User: Germany (Luftwaffe).

Development: The Heinkel 177, Germany's biggest bomber programme in World War II, is remembered as possibly the most troublesome and unsatisfactory aircraft in military history, and it was only through dogged courage and persistence that large numbers were put into service. Much of the fault lay in the stupid 1938 requirement that the proposed heavy bomber and anti-ship aircraft should be capable of dive bombing. Certainly the wish to reduce drag by using coupled pairs of engines was mistaken, because no engines in bomber history have caught fire so often in normal cruising flight. Six of the eight prototypes crashed and many of the 35 pre-production A-0s (built mainly by Arado) were written off in take-off swings

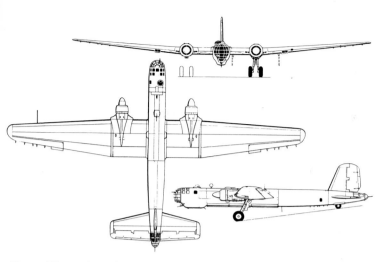

Above: Three-view of the first major variant, the He 177A-1/R1.

or in-flight fires. Arado built 130 A-1s, followed by 170 Heinkel-built A-3s and 826 A-5s with repositioned engines and longer fuselages. About 700 served on the Eastern Front, many having 50mm and 75mm guns for tank-busting; a few nervously bombed Britain in 400mph shallow dives, without any proper aiming of their bombs. So bothersome were these beasts that Goering forbade Heinkel to pester him any more with plans to use four separate engines, but Heinkel secretly flew the He 277, with four 1,750hp DB 603A, at Vienna, as the first of a major programme. The almost completely redesigned He 274 was a high-altitude bomber developed at the Farman factory at Suresnes, with four 1,850hp engines, a 145ft wing and twin fins. After the liberation it was readied for flight and flown at Orléans-Bricy.

Below: Main operational model was the A-5, of which 826 were built. This A-5/R2 has external racks for Fritz-X and Hs 293 guided missiles under its wings and on the centreline.

Ilyushin Il-4
TsKB-26, TsKB-30, DB-3 and DB-3F (Il-4)

Origin: Design bureau of Sergei Ilyushin, Soviet Union.
Type: Four-seat bomber and torpedo carrier.
Engines: Final standard, two 1,100hp M-88B 14-cylinder two-row radials.
Dimensions: Span 70ft 4¼in (21·44m); length 48ft 6½in (14·8m); height approximately 13ft 9in 4·2m).
Weights: About 13,230lb (6000kg); loaded 22,046lb (10,000kg).
Performance: Maximum speed 255mph (410km/h); initial climb 886ft (270m)/min; service ceiling 32,808ft (10,000m); range with 2,205lb of bombs 1,616 miles (2600km).
Armament: Three manually aimed machine guns, in nose, dorsal turret and periscopic ventral position, originally all 7·62mm ShKAS and from 1942 all 12·7mm BS; internal bomb bay for ten 220lb (100kg) bombs or equivalent, with alternative (or, for short ranges, additional) racks for up to three 1,102lb (500kg) or one 2,072lb (940kg) torpedo or one 2,205lb (1000kg) bomb, all under fuselage.
History: First flight (TsKB-26) 1935; (production DB-3) 1937; (DB-3F) 1939; final delivery 1944.
User: Soviet Union (DA, VMF).

Development: Though much less well-known around the world than such Western bombers as the B-17 and Lancaster, the Il-4 was one of the great bombers of World War II and saw service in enormous numbers in all roles from close support to strategic bombing of Berlin and low-level torpedo attacks. Originally known by its design bureau designation of TsKB-26 (often reported in the West as CKB-26), it was officially designated DB-3 (DB for Dalni Bombardirovshchik, long-range bomber) and went into production in early 1937. Powered by two 765hp M-85 engines, soon replaced by 960hp M-86, it was roughly in the class of the Hampden, with excellent speed, range, load and manoeuvrability but poor defensive armament (which was never changed, apart from increasing the calibre of the three guns). In 1939, when 1,528 had been delivered, production switched to the DB-3F with blunt nose turret replaced by a long pointed nose. In 1940, when over 2,000 were delivered, the designation was

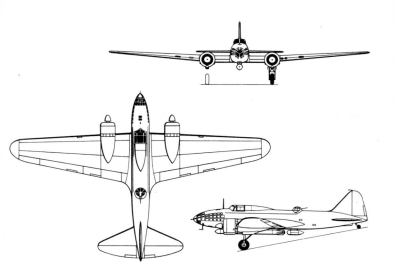

Above: Three-view of an Il-4 of the type used by the VVS-VMF for bombing and (as shown) torpedo attacks.

changed to Il-4, conforming with the new scheme in which aircraft were named for their designers (in this case Sergei Ilyushin). After the German invasion desperate materials shortage nearly halted production but by 1942 new plants in Siberia were building huge numbers of Il-4s with a redesigned airframe incorporating the maximum amount of wood. More than 6,800 had been delivered when production was stopped in 1944. Il-4s bombed Berlin many times, the first time by a force of VVS-VMF (Soviet Navy) Il-4s on 8 August 1941. By 1943 reconnaissance and glider towing were additional duties for these hard-worked aircraft.

Below: This was one of the many Il-4s used by the VVS-VMF, the Soviet naval air force. It could carry a weapon load of 2500kg.

Junkers Ju 86
Ju 86D, E, G, K, P and R

Origin: Junkers Flugzeug und Motorenwerke AG; also built by Henschel, and built under licence by Saab, Sweden.
Type: (D, E, G and K) bomber; (P) bomber/reconnaissance; (R) reconnaissance.
Engines: (D) two 600hp Junkers Jumo 205C six opposed-piston cylinder diesels; (E, G) two 800 or 880hp BMW 132 nine-cylinder radials; (K) two 905hp Bristol Mercury XIX nine-cylinder radials; (P, R) two 1,000hp Jumo 207A-1 or 207B-3/V turbocharged opposed-piston diesels.
Dimensions: Span 73ft 10in (22·6m); (P) 84ft (25·6m); (R) 105ft (32m); length (typical) 58ft 8½in (17·9m); (G) 56ft 5in; (P, R) 54ft; height (all) 15ft 5in (4·7m).
Weights: Empty (E-1) 11,464lb (5200kg); (R-1) 14,771lb (6700kg); loaded (E-1) 18,080lb (8200kg); (R-1) 25,420lb (11,530kg).
Performance: Maximum speed (E-1) 202mph (325km/h); (R-1) 261mph (420km/h); initial climb (E) 918ft (280m)/min; service ceiling (E-1) 22,310ft (6800m); (R-1) 42,650ft (13,000m); range (E) 746 miles (1200m); (R-1) 980 miles (1577km).
Armament: (D, E, G, K) three 7·92mm MG 15 manually aimed from nose, dorsal and retractable ventral positions; internal bomb load of four 551lb (250kg) or 16 110lb (50kg) bombs; (P) single 7·92mm fixed MG 17, same bomb load; (R) usually none.
History: First flight (Ju 86V-1) 4 November 1934; (V-5 bomber prototype) January 1936; (production D-1) late 1936; (P-series prototype) February 1940.
Users: Bolivia, Chile, Germany (Luftwaffe, Lufthansa), Hungary, Portugal, South Africa, Spain, Sweden.

Development: Planned like the He 111 as both a civil airliner and a bomber, the Ju 86 was in 1934 one of the most advanced aircraft in Europe. The design team under Dipl-Ing Zindel finally abandoned corrugated skin

Above: One of the colourful Ju 86K-2 bombers of the Hungarian 3./I Bombázó Oszatály, based at Tapolca in 1938.

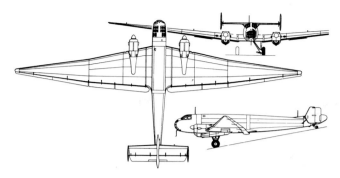

Above: Three-view of the extreme-altitude Ju 86R-1.

and created a smooth and efficient machine with prominent double-wing flaps and outward-retracting main gears. The diesel-engined D-1 was quickly put into Luftwaffe service to replace the Do 23 and Ju 52 as the standard heavy bomber, but in Spain the various· D-versions proved vulnerable even to biplane fighters. The E-series bombers, with the powerful BMW radial, were faster and the fastest of all were the Swedish Bristol-engined Ks, of which 40 were built by Junkers (first delivery 18 December 1936) and 16 by Saab (last delivery 3 January 1941). Many D and E bombers were used against Poland, but that was their swan-song. By 1939 Junkers was working on a high-altitude version with turbocharged engines and a pressure cabin and this emerged as the P-1 bomber and P-2 bomber/reconnaissance which was operational over the Soviet Union gathering pictures before the German invasion of June 1941. The R series had a span increased even beyond that of the P and frequently operated over southern England in 1941–2 until – with extreme difficulty – solitary Spitfires managed to reach their altitude and effect an interception. Total military Ju 86 production was between 810 and 1,000. Junkers schemed many developed versions, some having four or six engines.

Below: A Ju 86A-1 of KG 253 on manoeuvres in winter 1936-37, when this was still a very modern bomber. No guns are fitted to this aircraft, though the dustbin turret is extended.

Junkers Ju 188

Ju 188A, D and E series, and Ju 388, J, K and L

Origin: Junkers Flugzeug und Motorenwerke AG; with subcontract manufacture of parts by various French companies.

Type: Five-seat bomber (D-2, reconnaissance).

Engines: (Ju 188A) two 1,776hp Junkers Jumo 213A 12-cylinder inverted-vee liquid-cooled; (Ju 188D) same as A; (Ju 188E) two 1,700hp BMW 801G-2 18-cylinder two-row radials.

Dimensions: Span 72ft 2in (22m); length 49ft 1in (14·96m); height 16ft 1in (4·9m).

Weights: Empty (188E-1) 21,825lb (9900kg); loaded (188A and D) 33,730lb (15,300kg); (188E-1) 31,967lb (14,500kg).

Performance: Maximum speed (188A) 325mph (420km/h) at 20,500ft (6250m); (188D) 350mph (560km/h) at 27,000ft (8235m); (188E) 315mph (494km/h) at 19,685ft (6000m); service ceiling (188A) 33,000ft (10,060m); (188D) 36,090ft (11,000m); (188E) 31,170ft (9500m); range with 3,300lb (1500kg) bomb load (188A and E) 1,550 miles (2480km).

Armament: (A, D-1 and E-1) one 20mm MG 151/20 cannon in nose, one MG 151/20 in dorsal turret, one 13mm MG 131 manually aimed at rear dorsal position and one MG 131 or twin 7·92mm MG 81 manually aimed at rear ventral position; 6,614lb (3000kg) bombs internally or two 2,200lb (1000kg) torpedoes under inner wings.

History: First flight (Ju 88B-0) early 1940; (Ju 88V27) September 1941; (Ju 188V1) December 1941; (Ju 188E-1) March 1942; (Ju 388L) May 1944.

User: Germany (Luftwaffe).

Above: One of the best anti-shipping aircraft of World War II, the Ju 188E-2 was equipped with FuG 200 Hohentwiel radar and could carry two of the advanced LT 1B or LT F5b torpedoes. Not all E-2 aircraft had the EDL 131 dorsal turret, but the G even had a manned turret (with two MG 131s) in the extreme tail.

Right: Painted in 72/73 green shades with a wavy line of 65 light blue, this Ju 188D-2 operated from Kirkenes, Norway, in 1944 with 1(F)/124. The D-2 was a maritime reconnaissance aircraft with FuG 200 radar.

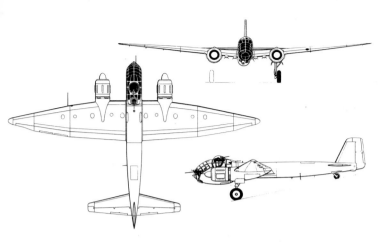

Above: Three-view of the Ju 188E-1 bomber, one of the versions with the BMW 801G-2 radial engine.

Development: In 1939 Junkers had the Jumo 213 engine in advanced development and, to go with it, the aircraft side of the company prepared an improved Ju 88 with a larger yet more streamlined crew compartment, more efficient pointed wings and large squarish tail. After protracted development this went into production as the Ju 188E-1, fitted with BMW 801s because the powerful Jumo was still not ready. The plant at Bernburg delivered 120 E-1s and a few radar-equipped turretless E-2s and reconnaissance F versions before, in mid-1943, finally getting into production with the A-1 version. Leipzig/Mockau built the A-2 with flame-damped exhaust for night operations and the A-3 torpedo bomber. The D was a fast reconnaissance aircraft, and the Ju 188S was a family of high-speed machines, for various duties, capable of up to 435mph (696km/h). Numerous other versions, some with a remotely controlled twin-MG 131 tail turret, led to the even faster and higher-flying Ju 388 family of night fighters (J), reconnaissance (L) and bomber aircraft (K). Altogether about 1,100 Ju 188 and about 120 388s were delivered, while at the war's end the much larger and markedly different Ju 288 had been shelved and the Ju 488, a much enlarged four-engined 388, had been built at Toulouse. All these aircraft, and the even greater number of stillborn projects, were evidence of the increasingly urgent need to make up for the absence of properly conceived new designs by wringing the utmost development out of the obsolescent types with which the Luftwaffe had started the war.

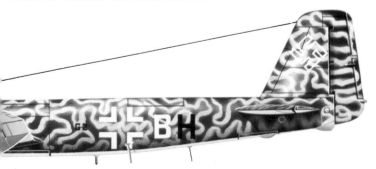

Junkers Ju 290

Ju 290A-1 to A-8 and B-1, B-2 and C

Origin: Junkers Flugzeug und Motorenwerke; design and development at Prague-Letnany, prototypes at Dessau and production at Bernberg.

Type: Long-range transport and reconnaissance bomber.

Engines: Four BMW 801 14-cylinder radials, (A) usually 1,700hp 801D, (B) 1,970hp 801E.

Dimensions: Span 137ft 9½in (42·00m); length 92ft 1in to 97ft 9in (A-5, 93ft 11½in, 28·64m); height 22ft 4¾in (6·83m).

Weights: Empty, not known (published figures cannot be correct); maximum (A-5) 99,141lb (44,970kg), (A-7) 101,413lb (45,400kg), (B-2) 111,332lb (50,500kg).

Performance: Maximum speed (all, without missiles) about 273mph (440km/h); maximum range (typical) 3,700 miles (5950km), (B-2) 4,970 miles (8000km).

Armament: See text.

History: First flight (rebuilt Ju 90V5) early 1939, (production 290A-0) October 1942; programme termination October 1944.

User: Germany (Luftwaffe).

Development: In 1936 Junkers considered the possibility of turning the Ju 89 strategic bomber into the Ju 90 airliner. With the death of Gen Wever the Ju 89 was cancelled and the Ju 90 became the pride of Deutsche Lufthansa. By 1937 the civil Ju 90S (Schwer = heavy) was in final design, with the powerful BMW 139 engine. By 1939 this had flown, with a new

Above: Taken at the Junkers plant at Bernburg, the centre for Ju 290 development, this shows the first production A-7 (Werk-Nr 0186) being readied for flight in May 1944.

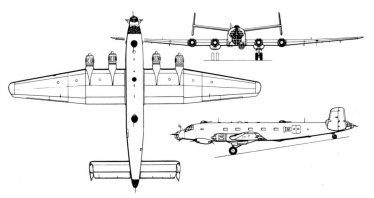

Above: Three-view of the Ju 290A-7 (photograph opposite).

wing and BMW 801 engines, and via a string of development prototypes led to the Ju 290A-0 and A-1 transports first used at Stalingrad. The A-2 was an Atlantic patrol machine, with typical armament of five 20mm MG 151 (including two power turrets) and six 13mm MG 131. There were many other versions, and the A-7 introduced a bulbous glazed nose; armament of the A-8 series was ten MG 151 and one (or three) MG 131, the most powerful carried by any bomber of World War II. The B carried more fuel and pressurized crew compartments, and like some A versions had radar and could launch Hs 293 and other air/surface missiles. In 1944 three A-5 made round trips to Manchuria.

Above: A Ju 290A-5 of FAGr 5 ocean-recon geschwader, 1943.

Below: The first Ju 290A-3 transport, also used by FAGr 5.

Kawasaki Ki-48 "Lily"

Ki-48-I, -IIa, -IIb and -IIc
(Allied code-name "Lily")

Origin: Kawasaki Kokuki Kogyo KK.
Type: Four-seat light bomber.
Engines: Two 14-cylinder radials, (-I) 980hp Nakajima Ha-25 (Army Type 99), (-II) 1,150hp Nakajima Ha-115 (Army Type 1).
Dimensions: Span 57ft 3¾in (17·47m); length (-I) 41ft 4in (12·60m), (-II) 41ft 10in (12·75m); height 12ft 5½in (3·80m).
Weights: Empty (-I) 8,928lb (4050kg), (-II) 10,030lb (4550kg); loaded (-I) 13,337lb (6050kg), (-II) 14,880lb (6750kg).
Performance: Maximum speed (-I) 298mph (480km/h), (-II) 314mph (505km/h); range (both, bomb load not specified) 1,491 miles (2400km).
Armament: (most) three 7·7mm Type 89 manually aimed from nose, dorsal and ventral positions, (-IIc) two Type 89 in nose, one ventral and manually aimed 12·7mm Type 1 dorsal; (all) internal bay for bomb load of up to 882lb (400kg), with normal load of 661lb (300kg) (-II capable of carrying 1,764lb, 800kg, but seldom used).
History: First flight July 1939; service delivery July or August 1940; final delivery October 1944.
User: Japan (Imperial Army).

Development: The Imperial Army's procurement organization tended to plan aircraft to meet existing, rather than future, threats. This straightforward bomber was requested in answer to the Soviet Union's SB-2. The latter was designed in 1933 and in action in Spain in 1936, but the Ki-48 (which was inferior in bomb load and only slightly faster) was a World War II machine. Entering service in China, it did well and proved popular, and it soon became the most important light bomber in the south-west Pacific with 557 -I built by June 1942. But its deficient performance and protection forced it to operate by night, which reduced the effectiveness of the small bomb load. The lengthened and more powerful -IIa had armour and protected tanks, and the -IIb had dive-bombing airbrakes; later examples of both had a dorsal fin. The -IIc had better armament, with provision also for machine guns fired

Lockheed Model 414 (A-29, PBO) Hudson

Hudson I to VI, A-28, A-29, AT-18, C-63 and PBO-1

Origin: Lockheed Aircraft Corporation.
Type: Reconnaissance bomber and utility.
Engines: (Hudson I, II) two 1,100hp Wright GR-1820-G102A nine-cylinder radials; (Hudson III, A-29, PBO-1) two 1,200hp GR-1820-G205A, (Hudson IV, V, VI and A-28) two 1,200hp Pratt & Whitney R-1830-S3C3-G, S3C4-G or -67 14-cylinder two-row radials.
Dimensions: Span 65ft 6in (19·96m); length 44ft 4in (13·51m); height 11ft 10½in (3·62m).
Weights: Empty (I) 12,000lb (5443kg); (VI) 12,929lb (5864kg); maximum loaded (I) 18,500lb (8393kg); (VI) 22,360lb (10,142kg).
Performance: Maximum speed (I) 246mph (397km/h); (VI) 261mph (420km/h); initial climb 1,200ft (366m)/min; service ceiling 24,500ft

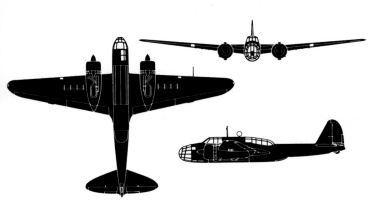

Above: Three-view of Ki-48-IIb (IIc similar).

Below: The Ki-48-IIb was fitted with snow-fence type dive-bombing airbrakes above and below the wings.

from each side of the nose, but the Ki-48 was inherently obsolete and after a total of 1,977 of all versions production stopped in 1944. Many were used for suicide attacks and as test-beds for missiles and the Ne-00 turbojet (carried on a pylon under the bomb bay).

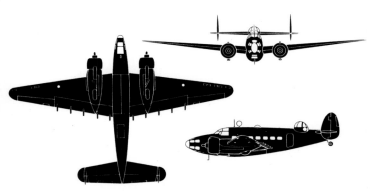

Above: Three-view of Hudson I (all Cyclone-powered similar).

(7468m); range (I) 1,960 miles (3150km); (VI) 2,160 miles (3475km).
Armament: (Typical RAF Hudson in GR role) seven 0·303in Brownings in nose (two, fixed), dorsal turret (two), beam windows and ventral hatch; internal bomb/depth charge load up to 750lb (341kg). *continued* ▶

History: First flight (civil Model 14) 29 July 1937; (Hudson I) 10 December 1938; squadron delivery February 1939; USAAC and USN delivery, October 1941.

Users: Australia, Brazil, Canada, China, Netherlands, New Zealand, UK (RAF, BOAC), US (AAC/AAF, Navy).

Development: In 1938 the British Purchasing Commission was established in Washington to seek out US aircraft that could serve with the RAF and Royal Navy and help bolster British strength beyond the then-small capacity of the British aircraft industry. One of the urgent needs was for a modern long-range reconnaissance and navigation trainer aircraft and Lockheed Aircraft, at Burbank — just climbing out of the Depression — hastily built a mock-up of their Model 14 airliner to meet the requirement. An order for 200 aircraft, many times bigger than any previous order ever received by

Right: One of a batch of 390 Lockheed Hudson GR.V reconnaissance-bombers delivered in 1940-41. This version had the two-row Twin Wasp engine with a long-chord cowling with cooling gills (seen fully open in the photograph below). Some of this batch went to the Middle East, some to the UK and some direct to New Zealand.

Below: As it was derived from a civil airliner the Hudson naturally made a good transport, and it was in this role that the majority were eventually used (though many stayed in action with such later extras as radar and underwing rocket rails). This is a GR.VI, which despite the general-recon designation was serving in West Africa on transport duties from 1941 onwards. Note the open bomb doors.

Lockheed, was fulfilled swiftly and efficiently. The order was many times multiplied and the versatile Hudson served with several RAF commands in many theatres of war. On 8 October 1939 a Hudson over Jutland shot down the first German aircraft claimed by the RAF in World War II. In February 1940 another discovered the prison ship *Altmark* in a Norwegian fjord and directed naval forces to the rescue. Over Dunkirk Hudsons acted as dog-fighters, in August 1941 one accepted the surrender of U-boat *U-570*, and from 1942 many made secret landings in France to deliver or collect agents or supplies. Hudsons of later marks carried ASV radar, rocket launchers and lifeboats. Total deliveries were 2,584 including about 490 armed versions for the US Army, 20 PBOs for the Navy and 300 AT-18 crew trainers. From this fine basic design stemmed the more powerful Vega Ventura bomber and ocean patrol aircraft and the PV-2 Harpoon at almost twice the weight of the Hudson I.

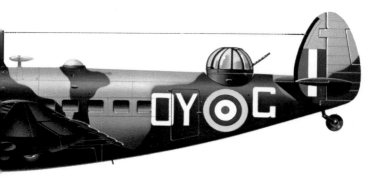

Lockheed PV-1/B-34 Ventura
Vega 37, Ventura I to V, B-34 Lexington, B-37, PV-1 and -3 and PV-2 Harpoon

Origin: Vega Aircraft Corporation, Burbank, California.
Type: Bomber and reconnaissance aircraft.
Engines: Two Pratt & Whitney R-2800 Double Wasp 18-cylinder radials, (Ventura I) 1,850hp R-2800-S1A4-G, (most others) 2,000hp R-2800-31.
Dimensions: Span 65ft 6in (19·96m), (H) 75ft 0in (22·86m); length 51ft 5in to 51ft 9in (15·77m); height 13ft 2in to 14ft 1in (4·29m).
Weights: Empty (PV-1, typical) 19,373lb (8788kg), (H) about 24,000lb (10,886kg); maximum (V) 31,077lb (14,097kg), (H) 40,000lb (18,144kg).
Performance: Maximum speed (V) 300mph (483km/h), (H) 282mph (454km/h); maximum range with max bomb load (all) about 900 miles (1448km).
Armament: See text.
History: First flight (RAF) 31 July 1941; service delivery (RAF) June 1942; final delivery (H) 1945.
Users: (WWII) Australia, Italy (CB), New Zealand, Portugal, South Africa, UK (RAF), US (AAF, Navy).

Development: Vega Aircraft, a 1940 subsidiary of Lockheed, was awarded a contract by the British Purchasing Commission in June 1940 for 875 of a new design of bomber derived from the Lockheed 18 airliner. Called Lockheed V-146, or Vega 37, it resembled a more powerful Hudson, with

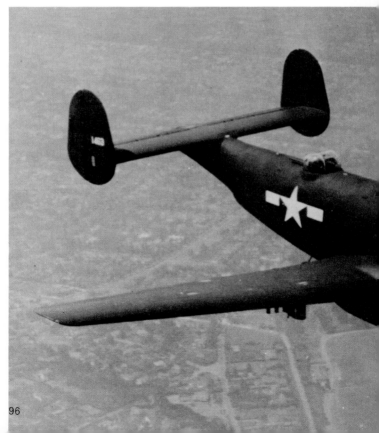

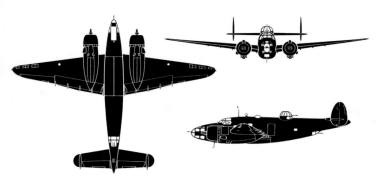

Above: Three-view of all Venturas (B-34 similar).

longer fuselage provided with a rear ventral position with two 0·303in Brownings. Two (later four) more were in the dorsal turret, and the nose had two fixed 0·5in and two manually aimed 0·303in. Bomb load was 2,500lb (1134kg). In October 1942 Bomber Command's No 21 Sqn swept into action with a gallant daylight attack on the Phillips works at Eindhoven, but the Ventura proved a mediocre bomber and deliveries stopped at about ▶

Below: Final model of the 14/Hudson/Ventura family, the PV2 Harpoon was redesigned with a new wing and tail and many other changes, including three extra nose guns under the new radar.

300. The B-34 Lexington absorbed many of the unwanted machines, though the Army Air Force never used them operationally. The B-34B trainer, Ventura II and IIA were reconnaissance models (originally O-56), but the bulk of the 1,600 Venturas were Navy PV-1 patrol bombers with up to eight 0·5in, more fuel and ability to carry mines and torpedoes. About 380 similar aircraft served Commonwealth forces as Ventura V, surviving in South Africa to the 1970s. The PV-2 Harpoon was redesigned as a much better Navy bomber, with larger wings, new tail and up to ten 0·5in, rockets and 4,000lb (1814kg) of bombs or torpedoes. The 535 built saw brief service before being passed to Allies.

Right: This PV-1 Ventura patrol bomber of the US Navy was photographed at the Vega plant mounted on a rotatable platform having its compass swung. By 1943 many PVs had ASV radar.

Martin 167 Maryland

Model 167 Maryland I and II

Origin: The Glenn L. Martin Company.
Type: Three-seat reconnaissance bomber.
Engines: Two Pratt & Whitney Twin Wasp 14-cylinder two-row radials; (Maryland I) 1,050hp R-1830-S1C3-G; (II) 1,200hp R-1830-S3C4-G.
Dimensions: Span 61ft 4in (18·69m); length 46ft 8in (14·22m); height 10ft 1in (3·07m).
Weights: Empty 11,213lb (RAF Mk II); maximum loaded (I) 15,297lb; (II) 16,809lb (7694kg).
Performance: Maximum speed (prototype) 316mph; (I) 304mph; (II) 280mph (451km/h); initial climb 1,790ft (545m)/min; service ceiling (I) 29,500ft (8992m); (II) 26,000ft (7925m); range with bomb load 1,080 miles (1738km).
Armament: Four 0·303in Browning (France, 7·5mm MAC 1934) fixed in outer wings, two 0·303in Vickers K (France, MAC 1934) manually aimed

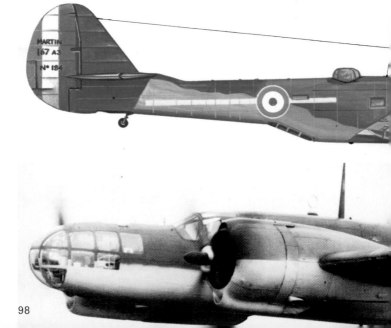

from dorsal turret and rear ventral position; internal bomb load of 2,000lb (907kg) (France 1,874lb, 850kg; Maryland I, 1,250lb, 567kg).
History: First flight 14 March 1939; (production 167F) 7 August 1939; service delivery (France) October 1939; final delivery 1941.
Users: France, South Africa, UK (RAF, RN).

Development: Designed as the US Army XA-22 attack bomber, the Martin 167 was not adopted but immediately attracted a big French order for the Armée de l'Air as the 167F, with Armée de l'Air designation 167A-3. Of 215 purchased, about 75 reached France before the June 1940 capitulation, squadrons GB I/62 and I/63 completing conversion and, despite being chosen for dangerous missions, suffering only 8 per cent casualties (the lowest of any French bomber type). Some survivors and undelivered aircraft went to the RAF, while most surviving French aircraft served the Vichy Air Force and operated against the Allies over Gibraltar, North Africa and Syria. The RAF accepted 75 ex-French machines and bought a further 150 with two-stage supercharged engines as the Maryland II, using all 225 as reconnaissance bombers in Cyrenaica, Malta and other Middle East areas. A few went to the Fleet Air Arm (one gave first warning of the departure of *Bismarck*) and four squadrons served with the South African AF. In basic arrangement rather like Luftwaffe bombers, the Maryland was quite fast, nice to fly, but cramped and inadequately armed.

Left: This aircraft, designated Martin 167A-3 by the French, was used by GB I/63 of the Vichy forces against Gibraltar.

Below: The first Maryland I, built to a French order and taken over by the RAF. This mark had US equipment.

Martin 179 B-26 Marauder
Model 179, B-26A to G, Marauder I to III

Origin: The Glenn L. Martin Company.
Type: Five- to seven-seat medium bomber.
Engines: Two Pratt & Whitney Double Wasp 18-cylinder two-row radials;
(B-26) 1,850hp R-2800-5; (A) 2,000hp R-2800-39; (B, C, D, E, F, G)
2,000hp R-2800-43.
Dimensions: Span (B-26, A and first 641 B-26B) 65ft (19·8m); (remainder) 71ft (21·64m); length (B-26) 56ft, (A, B) 58ft 3in (17·75m);
(F, G) 56ft 6in (17·23m); height (up to E) 19ft 10in (6·04m); (remainder)
21ft 6in (6·55m).
Weights: Empty (early, typical) 23,000lb (10,433kg); (F, G) 25,300lb
(11,490kg); maximum loaded (B-26) 32,000lb; (A) 33,022lb; (first 641 B)
34,000lb, then 37,000lb (16,783kg); (F) 38,000lb (G) 38,200lb (17,340kg).
Performance: Maximum speed (up to E, typical) 310mph (500km/h); (F,
G) 280mph (451km/h); initial climb 1,000ft (305m)/min; service ceiling
(up to E) 23,000ft (7000m); (F, G) 19,800ft (6040m); range with 3,000lb
(1361kg) bomb load (typical) 1,150 miles (1850km).
Armament: (B-26, A) five 0·30in or 0·50in Browning in nose (1 or 2),
power dorsal turret (2), tail (1, manual) and optional manual ventral
hatch; (B to E) one 0·5in manually aimed in nose, twin-gun turret, two
manually aimed 0·5in waist guns, one "tunnel gun" (usually 0·5in), two
0·5in in power tail turret and four 0·5in fixed as "package guns" on sides of
forward fuselage; (F, G) same but without tunnel gun; some variations and
trainer and Navy versions unarmed. Internal bomb load of 5,200lb (2359kg)
up to 641st B, after which rear bay was disused (eliminated in F, G) to give
maximum load of 4,000lb (1814kg). Early versions could carry two
torpedoes.
History: First flight 25 November 1940; service delivery 25 February 1941;
final delivery March 1945.
Users: France, South Africa, UK (RAF), US (AAF, Navy).

Development: With its background of leadership in bomber design,
Martin pulled out all the stops to win the 1939 Medium Bomber competition
of the US Army, and boldly chose a wing optimised for high-speed cruise
efficiency rather than for landing. Though the Model 179 won the competition — 201 being ordered "off the drawing board" on 5 July 1939 — the
actual hardware proved too much for inexperienced pilots to handle, with
unprecedented wing loading. In fact there were no real problems, but the
newness of the first B-26 versions, coupled with their reputation of being a

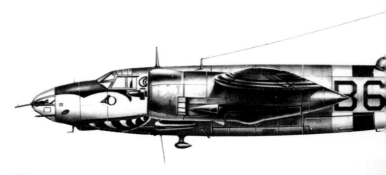

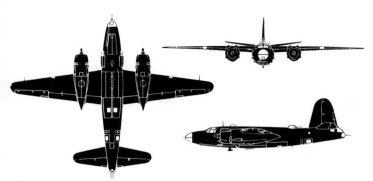

Above: Three-view of B-26C (Marauder III similar).

"widow maker", created a vicious circle of high casualties. Production
B-26A models, with torpedo shackles between the bomb doors, were
deployed to Australia the day after Pearl Harbor (8 December 1941), and
later B models saw extensive South West Pacific service with the rear bomb
bay used as a fuel tank (maximum bomb load 2,000lb). From the 641st B
the wing and vertical tail were extended and on 14 May 1943 the Marauder
began its career as the chief medium bomber of the 9th AF in the ETO
(European Theatre of Operations). By VE-day the B-26 had set a record for
the lowest loss-rate of any US Army bomber in Europe. About 522 also ▶

Above: Among the lesser-known sub-
types of Marauder were the JM-1 target
tugs of the US Navy, which were painted
yellow. The Navy had 225 JM-1s (ex-
USAAF AT-23B crew trainers converted
from B-26Cs, as illustrated) and 47 JM-2s
converted from the TB-26G.

Left: By far the most important B-26
operator in Europe was the 9th Air Force,
whose B-26s served alongside the A-20
and new A-26 Invader in pounding enemy
targets by day. This B-26B-55, painted in
D-day invasion stripes, was assigned to
the 9th AAF 397th Bombardment Group.

served with the RAF and South African AF in Italy. Total production amounted to 5,157 for the US Army (including Allied forces) plus a few dozen JM-1 and -2 target tug, reconnaissance and utility versions for the US Navy and about 200 AT-23 (later called TB-26) trainers. In 1948 the Marauder was withdrawn, and the B-26 designation passed to the Douglas Invader.

Above: A B-26B-55, one of a formation of various Marauder sub-types heading out over Florence to bomb Kesselring's Italian front.

Below: A Bomb Group of the 8th (not the 9th) Army Air Force streaming round a taxiway in southern England for a mission in 1944. As far as can be seen, the aircraft are B-26Cs.

Martin 187 Baltimore
Model 187, Baltimore I to V
(US Army A-30)

Origin: The Glenn L. Martin Company.
Type: Four-seat light bomber.
Engines: Two Wright Cyclone 14-cylinder two-row radials; (I, II) 1,600hp R-2600-A5B; (III, IV) 1,660hp R-2600-19; (V) 1,700hp R-2600-29.
Dimensions: Span 61ft 4in (18·69m); length 48ft 6in (14·78m); height 17ft 9in (5·41m).
Weights: Empty (III) 15,200lb (6895kg); maximum loaded (I) 22,958lb; (III) 23,000lb (10,433kg); (V) 27,850lb (12,632kg).
Performance: Maximum speed (I) 308mph; (III, IV) 302mph; (V) 320mph (515km/h); initial climb 1,500ft (457m)/min; service ceiling (typical) 24,000ft (7315m); range with 1,000lb bomb load (typical) 1,060 miles (1700km).
Armament: Four 0·303in Brownings fixed in outer wings; mid-upper position with manually aimed 0·303in Vickers K (I), twin Vickers (II), Boulton Paul turret with two or four 0·303in Browning (III), Martin turret with two 0·5in Browning (IV, V); rear ventral position with two 0·303in

Right: Seldom hitting the headlines, the Baltimore worked hard by day and night from Libya through Tunisia and Sicily to Italy and the Balkans. This formation of Mk V (ex-USAAF A-30) bombers belonged to the Italian Stormo Baltimore, a major element of the Co-Belligerent AF formed in early 1943.

Below: Another Co-Belligerent Baltimore (a Mk IV or V) is seen in this photograph taken on an Italian airfield in early 1944.

Vickers K; optional four or six fixed 0·303in guns firing directly to rear or obliquely downward. Internal bomb load up to 2,000lb (907kg).

History: First flight 14 June 1941; service delivery October 1941; final delivery May 1944.

Users: Australia, France, Italy, South Africa, Turkey, UK (RAF, RN).

Development: Martin received an RAF order in May 1940 for 400 improved Maryland bombers with deeper fuselages to allow intercommunication between crew members. In the course of design the more powerful R-2600 engine was adopted and the final aircraft marked an appreciable all-round improvement. The 400 were made up of 50 Mk I, 100 Mk II and 250 Mk III differing mainly in mid-upper armament. To facilitate Lend-Lease contracts, under which additional machines were ordered, the Model 187 was given the US Army designation A-30, but none were supplied for American use. After 281 Mk IIIA, identical to the III but on US Lend-Lease account, and 294 Mk IV, production completed with 600 Mk V (A-30A), the total being 1,575 all for the RAF. Many were passed on to the South African AF, and a few to the Royal Navy, all being worked very hard in Cyrenaica, Tunisia, Sicily and Italy in bombing and close-support missions. In 1944 units of the co-belligerent Italian forces received ex-RAF machines and formed the Stormo Baltimore which was active over Jugoslavia and the Balkans.

Mitsubishi G3M "Nell"

G3M1, G3M2 and G3M3; some rebuilt as L3Y

Origin: Mitsubishi Jukogyo KK, Nagoya; also built by Nakajima Hikoki KK at Koizumi.

Type: Long-range land-based bomber (L3Y, transport).

Engines: Two Mitsubishi Kinsei 14-cylinder two-row radials, (G3M1, L3Y1) 910hp Kinsei 3, (G3M2, L3Y2) 1,075hp Kinsei 42 or 45, (G3M3) 1,300hp Kinsei 51.

Dimensions: Span 82ft 0¼in (25·00m); length 53ft 11½in (16·45m); height 12ft 1in (3·685m).

Weights: Empty (1) 10,516lb (4770kg), (3) 11,551lb (5243kg); max loaded (1) 16,848lb (7642kg), (3) 17,637lb (8000kg).

Performance: Maximum speed (1) 216mph (348km/h), (2) 232mph (373km/h), (3) 258mph (415km/h); service ceiling (3) 33,730ft (10,280 m); maximum range (3) 3,871 miles (6228km).

Armament: (1 and 2) up to four 7·7mm Type 92 manually aimed from two retractable dorsal positions, ventral position and cockpit, (3) one 20mm Type 99 in dorsal fairing and three 7.7mm in side blisters, and retractable dorsal turret; external bomb load or torpedo of 1,764lb (800kg).

History: First flight (Ka-15 prototype) July 1935; service delivery late 1936.

User: Imperial Japanese Navy.

Development: Derived from the Ka-9 of April 1934, the Ka-15 series ot prototypes were among the first outstanding Japanese warplanes superior to Western types. Designed by a team under Prof Kiro Honjo, the Ka-15 was

Right: Mitsubishi G3M2 bombers, probably of the Mihoro Kokutái, photographed whilst releasing their bombs in a stick. All aircraft in the picture are of the Model 22 sub-type with a large turtle-back dorsal gun position equipped with a 20mm cannon. The Mihoro Kokutai provided high-level bombers which sank the British capital ships _Prince of Wales_ and _Repulse_ on 10 December 1941.

Below: A formation of G3M3 bombers (the final G3M3 sub-type, the Model 22 had similar armament) with dorsal turrets extended and machine gun deployed ahead of the prominent dorsal canopy over the gunner who manned the cannon. Note the landing wheel on the nearest aircraft, which only retracted partially.

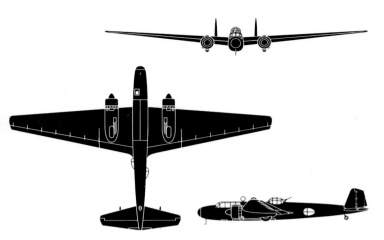

Above: Three-view of G3M3 Model 23 (G3M2 similar).

a smooth stressed-skin machine, with exceptional range. On 14 August 1937 the Kanoya air corps based on Taipei made the world's first trans-oceanic raid when a large force of G3M2 hit targets 1,250 miles away in China. Many other great raids were made, but the most famous action was the sinking of HMS *Prince of Wales* and *Repulse* (which thought they were out of range) on 10 December 1941. By 1943 most were in second-line service, though known to the Allies as "Nell". The L3Y transport conversion was code-named "Tina".

Mitsubishi G4M "Betty"

G4M1 to G4M3c and G6M

Origin: Mitsubishi Jukogyo KK.

Type: Land-based naval torpedo bomber and missile carrier.

Engines: (G4M1) two 1,530hp Mitsubishi Kasei 11 14-cylinder two-row radials; (subsequent versions) two Kasei 22 rated at 1,850hp with water/methanol injection.

Dimensions: Span 81ft 7¾in (24·89m); length (1) 65ft 6¼in; (later versions) 64ft 4¾in (19·63m); height (1) 16ft 1in; (later versions) 13ft 5¾in (4·11m).

Weights: Empty (1) 14,860lb (6741kg); (2) 17,623lb (7994kg); (3) 18,500lb (8391kg); loaded (1) 20,944lb (9500kg); (2, 3) 27,550lb (12,500kg); max overload (1) 28,350lb (12,860kg); (2, 3) 33,070lb (15,000kg).

Performance: Maximum speed (1) 265mph (428km/h); (2) 271mph (437km/h); (3) 283mph (455km/h); initial climb (1) 1,800ft (550m)/min; (2, 3) 1,380ft (420m)/min; service ceiling (all) about 30,000ft (9144m); range (with bombs at overload weight) (1) 3,132 miles (5040km); (2) 2,982 miles (4800km); (3) 2,262 miles (3640km).   *continued* ▶

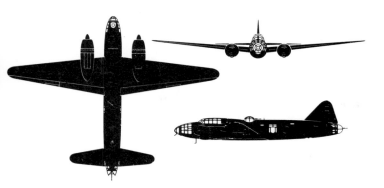

Above: Three-view of G4M2, without bulged weapon-bay doors.

Left: A G4M2a of the 763rd Kokutai (Air Corps). This aircraft was found abandoned in the Philippines. Finish was dark green above and natural metal on underside.

Below: Aircrew of a Navy kokutai (air corps) photographed near the end of World War II when the desperate situation had led to widespread suicide missions. The aircraft is a G4M2e carrying an MXY-7 Ohka piloted missile under its belly.

Armament: (1) three manually aimed 7·7mm in nose, dorsal and ventral positions and 20mm manually aimed in tail; internal bomb load of 2,205lb (1000kg) or 1,764lb (800kg) torpedo externally; (2) as before but electric dorsal turret (one 7·7mm) and revised tail position with increased arc of fire; (2e, and, retro-actively, many earlier G4M2) one 7·7mm in nose, one 20mm in dorsal turret and manual 20mm in tail and two beam windows. (G4M2e) adapted to carry Ohka piloted missile.

History: First flight October 1939; service delivery April 1941; first flight (G4M2) November 1942.

User: Japan (Imperial Navy).

Development: Designed to an incredibly difficult 1938 Navy specification, the G4M family (Allied name, "Betty") was the Imperial Japanese Navy's premier heavy bomber in World War II; yet the insistence on the great range of 2,000 nautical miles (3706km) with full bomb load made the saving of weight take priority over defence and the aircraft was highly vulnerable and not very popular. The wing was of the same Mitsubishi 118 section as the Zero-Sen and boldly designed as an integral fuel tank to accommodate no less than 5,000 litres (1,100gal). The company kept recommending four engines and being overruled by the Navy, which, during the early flight-test stage, wasted more than a year, and 30 aircraft, in trying to make the design into the G6M bomber escort with crew of ten and 19 guns. Eventually the G4M1 was readied for service as a bomber and flew its first missions in South East China in May 1941. More than 250 operated in the Philippines and Malayan campaigns, but after the Solomons battle in August 1942 it began to be apparent that, once intercepted and hit, the unprotected bomber went up like a torch (hence the Allied nickname "one-shot lighter").

Mitsubishi Ki-21 "Sally"

Ki-21-I, -IIa and -IIb

Origin: Mitsubishi Jukogyo KK; also built by Nakajima Hikoki KK.

Type: Seven-seat heavy bomber.

Engines: (I) two 850hp Nakajima Ha-5-Kai 14-cylinder two-row radials; (II) two 1,490hp Mitsubishi Ha-101 of same layout.

Dimensions: Span 73ft 9¾in (22·5m); length 52ft 6in (16·0m); height 15ft 11in (4·85m).

Weights: Empty (I) 10,341lb (4691kg); (II) 13,382lb (6070kg); maximum loaded (I) 16,517lb (7492kg); (II) 21,395lb (9710kg).

Performance: Maximum speed (I) 268mph (432km/h); (II) 297mph (478km/h); initial climb (I) 1,150ft (350m)/min; (II) 1,640ft (500m)/min; service ceiling (I) 28,220ft (8600m); (II) 32,800ft (10,000m); range with full bomb load (I) 1,678 miles (2700km); (II) 1,370 miles (2200km).

Armament: See text for defensive armament; internal bomb bay in fuselage for load of (I) 1,653lb (750kg) or (II) 2,205lb (1000kg).

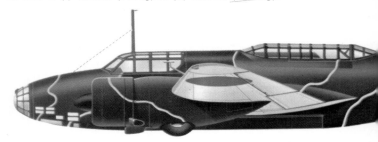

Above: Dark green and sky grey G4M1s over China in 1941.

Total production reached the exceptional quantity of 2,479, most of them in the many sub-types of G4M2 with increased fuel capacity and power. Finally the trend of development was reversed with the G4M3 series with full protection and only 968gal fuel.

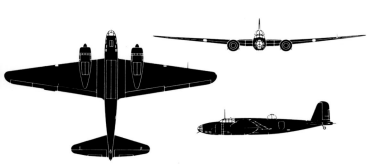

Above: Three-view of the Ki-21-IIb.

Left: This Ki-21-Ia of the 2nd Chutai, 60th Hikosentai, was painted in one of the more colourful Army finishes in which upper surfaces were olive green and brown separated by white strips, the undersurfaces of wings and tail-plane being light grey (rather like the Navy sky grey). In 1937, when this initial version entered service, the Ki 21 outperformed every other bomber except the B-17 then also just entering service. After Pearl Harbor, however, it was gradually recognised as obsolescent, though production continued until September 1944.

History: First flight November 1936; service delivery 1937; first flight (Ki-21-II) mid-1940; final delivery September 1944.
User: Japan (Imperial Army).

Development: In 1936 the Imperial Japanese Army issued a challenging specification for a new heavy bomber, demanding a crew of at least four, an endurance of five hours, a bomb load of 750kg and speed of 400km/h. Mitsubishi won over the Nakajima Ki-19 and built five prototypes powered by the company's own A.14 (Kinsei Ha-6) engine. The fields of fire of the three manually aimed 7·7mm machine guns were inadequate and the Army also requested a switch to the Ha-5 engine. With various modifications it was accepted as the Type 97 (also called OB-97; omoshi bakudanki meaning heavy bomber) and put into production not only by Mitsubishi but also, in 1938, by Nakajima. It rapidly became the premier Japanese Army heavy bomber and served throughout the "Chinese incident", the operational results being efficiently fed back to the procurement machine and the manufacturer. This led to the defensive armament being increased to five guns, one remotely controlled in the extreme tail, the crew being increased to seven. The bomb bay was enlarged, the flaps were increased in size and crew armour was dramatically augmented. The result was the Ki-21-Ib. Increase in fuel capacity and addition of a sixth (beam) gun resulted in the -Ic variant. In 1939 work began on the much more powerful -II, with increased-span tailplane. Several hundred of both versions were in use in December 1941 and they were met on all fronts in the Pacific war (being fairly easy meat for Hurricanes in Burma). Code-named "Sally" they faded from front-line service in 1943, though the -IIb with "glasshouse" replaced by a dorsal turret (one 12·7mm) improved defence when it entered service in 1942. Total production was 2,064 (351 by Nakajima), plus 500 transport versions (called MC-20, Ki-57 and "Topsy").

Below: Taken over Japan in 1941 or 1942, this photograph shows Ki-21-IIa bombers of the Hammamatsu Bomber School whose emblem appears on the tail of the nearest machine. As this model had no turret its chief role must have been to train pilots, navigators and bomb-aimers.

Above: After 1942 Japan had lost air supremacy almost everywhere and even front-line bombers such as this Ki-21-IIb of the 14th Sentai had to hug the treetops to try to evade Allied fighters. This olive green and light grey machine, with scarlet tail badge, was over the Philippines in 1944.

Mitsubishi Ki-30 "Ann"

Ki-30

Origin: Mitsubishi Jukogyo KK; also built by Tachikawa Dai-Ichi Rikugun Kokusho.
Type: Two-seat light bomber.
Engine: One 950hp Mitsubishi Ha-5 Zuisei 14-cylinder two-row radial.
Dimensions: Span 47ft 8¾in (14·55m); length 33ft 11in (10·34m) height 11ft 11¾in (3·65m).
Weights: Empty 4,915lb (2230kg); maximum loaded 7,324lb (3322kg).
Performance: Maximum speed 263mph (423km/h); initial climb 1,640ft (500m)/min; service ceiling 28,117ft (8570m); range (bomb load not stated) 1,056 miles (1700km).
Armament: One 7·7mm Type 89 machine gun fixed in wing (sometimes both wings) and one manually aimed from rear cockpit; internal bomb bay for three 220lb (100kg) or equivalent bomb load.
History: First flight February 1937; service delivery October 1938; final delivery 1941.
Users: Japan (Imperial Army), Thailand.

Development: With the Ki-32, Ki-27 fighter and Ki-21 heavy bomber, the Ki-30 was one of the important new stressed-skin monoplanes ordered by the Imperial Army under its modernisation plan of 1935. It was the first in Japan to have a modern two-row engine, as well as internal bomb bay, flaps and constant-speed propeller. It was notably smaller than the otherwise similar Fairey Battle produced in Britain. Unlike the British bomber the bomb bay was in the fuselage, resulting in a mid-wing and long landing gear (which was fixed). The pilot and observer/bomb aimer had a good view but were unable to communicate except by speaking tube. The Ki-30 was in service in numbers in time to be one of the major types in the Sino-Japanese war. In 1942 surviving aircraft played a large part in the advance to the Philippines, but then swiftly withdrew from first-line operations. Mitsubishi built 638 at Nagoya and 68 were completed at the Tachikawa Army Air Arsenal. In conformity with the Allied system of code-naming bombers after girls, the Ki-30 was dubbed "Ann". It was the ultimate development of the Karigane family of high-performance monoplanes. In the mid-1930s these had been the epitome of advanced technology, and until 1941 resulted in effective, reliable warplanes, but after that year the concept was obsolescent, and vulnerable to Allied fighters.

Left: A Ki-30 of the 2nd Chutai of the 10th Hikosentai. This was an excellent light bomber in the war against China, and saw much action in that theatre. From 1940 many were supplied to the Royal Thai Air Force for use against the Vichy French forces in Indo-China in a campaign begun in January 1941.

Below: Pilots and observers of a Ki-30 Chutai relax before a combat mission, probably in China before the start of World War II. At this period the Army painted its bombers pale grey or left them in natural metal finish. Note the projecting tube ahead of the spinner for the traditional Hucks starter.

Mitsubishi Ki-67 Hiryu "Peggy"

Ki-67-la, lb and II and Ki-109

Origin: Mitsubishi Jukogyo KK; also built by Kawasaki and (assembly only) Nippon Kokusai Koku Kogyo KK, plus one by Tachikawa.

Type: Heavy bomber and torpedo dropper; Ki-109 heavy escort fighter.

Engines: Two 1,900hp Mitsubishi Ha-104 18-cylinder two-row radials.

Dimensions: Span 73ft 9¾in (22·5m); length 61ft 4¼in (18·7m); height 18ft 4½in (5·60m).

Weights: (lb) empty 19,068lb (8649kg); loaded 30,346lb (13,765kg).

Performance: (lb) Maximum speed 334mph (537km/h); initial climb 1,476ft (450m)/min; service ceiling 31,070ft (9470m); range with full bomb load 621 miles (1000km) plus 2hr reserve, also reported as total range 1,740 miles (2800km).

Armament: Standard on la, lb, one 20mm Ho-5 in electric dorsal turret and single 12·7mm Type 1 manually aimed from nose, tail and two beam positions; internal bomb load 1,764lb (800kg); suicide attack 6,393lb (2900kg).

History: First flight "beginning of 1943"; service delivery April 1944; first flight (Ki-109) August 1944.

User: Japan (Imperial Army and Navy).

Development: Designed by a team led by Dr Hisanojo Ozawa to meet a February 1941 specification, this Army bomber not only met the demand for much higher speed but also proved to have the manoeuvrability of a fighter. It also lacked nothing in armour and fuel-tank protection, and was probably the best all-round bomber produced in Japan during World War II. With a crew of six/eight, it was often looped and shown to have excellent turning power, better than that of several Japanese fighters. Indeed the Ki-69 escort fighter version was developed in parallel with the bomber

Below: This Ki-67-lb was painted dark olive and pale grey and was serving with the 74th Sentai in 1944.

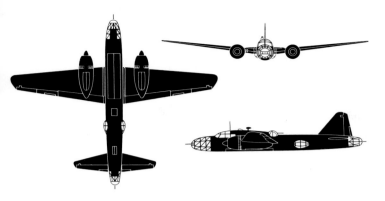

Above: Three-view of Ki-67-Ib.

during 1942 but had to be shelved as delays to the bomber were becoming serious. These delays were due to inefficiency, material shortage and continual changes requested by the customer. By 1944 only 15 (all different) had been built, but production was then allowed to begin in earnest and by VJ-day the creditable total of 727 had been delivered, 606 by Mitsubishi and the rest by Kawasaki, Nippon and (one only) the Tachikawa arsenal. At first the Ki-67 Hiryu (Flying Dragon) was used as a torpedo bomber in the Philippine Sea battle, receiving the Allied name "Peggy". Later it operated against Iwo Jima, the Marianas and Okinawa and in the defence of Japan. There were only two versions used, the Ib having bulged waist blisters. Of many projected versions, of which the Ki-67-II with 2,500hp Ha-214 engines marked the biggest advance, only the Ki-109 reached the service trials stage. Armed with a 75mm gun with 15 hand-loaded rounds, plus a 12·7mm in the tail, this was meant to have 2,000hp turbocharged Ha-104 engines but none were available. With ordinary Ha-104s the Ki-109 could not get up to B-29 altitude!

Below: This Mitsubishi Ki-67-Ib is in the hands of a combat unit but does not appear to have been painted in unit markings and may be new from the manufacturer. In general the Ki-67 was an excellent aircraft, and extremely popular with its crews, though internal bomb load was surprisingly small.

Nakajima Ki-49 Donryu "Helen"

Ki-49-I, IIa, IIb, III and Ki-58

Origin: Nakajima Hikoki KK; also built by Tachikawa Hikoki KK and (few) Mansyu Hikoki.

Type: Eight-seat heavy bomber; Ki-58, escort fighter.

Engines: (I) two 1,250hp Nakajima Ha-41 14-cylinder two-row radials; (II) two 1,450hp Nakajima Ha-109-II of same layout; (III) two 2,500hp Nakajima Ha-117 18-cylinder two-row radials.

Dimensions: Span 66ft 7¼in (20·3m); length 53ft 1⅜in (16·2m); height 13ft 11½in (4·25m).

Weights: Empty (II) 15,653lb (7100kg); normal loaded 23,545lb (10,680kg).

Performance: Maximum speed (II) 304mph (490km/h); initial climb 1,312ft (400m)/min; service ceiling 26,772ft (8160m); range with bomb load, 1,491 miles (2400km).

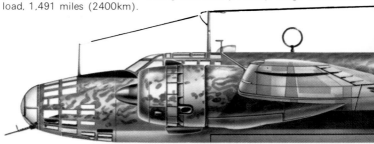

Armament: (I) one 20mm cannon manually aimed in dorsal position, single 7·7mm manually aimed at nose and tail; (IIa) as (I) plus extra 7·7mm in ventral and two beam positions (total five); (IIb) as IIa but with all 7·7mm replaced by 12·7mm, thus 20mm dorsal and single 12·7mm in nose, tail, ventral and two beam positions; all versions, internal bay for bomb load up to 2,205lb (1,000kg).

History: First flight August 1939; (production Ki-49-I) probably May 1940; (II) 1942; final delivery December 1944.

User: Japan (Imperial Army).

Development: Designed to a late 1938 specification aimed at replacing the Mitsubishi Ki-21, the Ki-49 was the first Japanese bomber to mount a 20mm cannon; but it was at first only slightly faster than the Ki-21, had a poor ceiling and never did achieve any advance in range and bomb load. The 1,160hp Nakajima Ha-5B engines of the prototype were replaced by the Ha-41, and 129 of the -I model were built at Ohta, after whose Donryu (Dragon Swallower) shrine the type was named. The production machine was the Type 100 heavy bomber, and the Allied code name was "Helen". Its first mission was a raid on Port Darwin from a New Guinea base on 19 February 1942. The main model was the better-armed -II series, of which 649 were made by Nakajima, 50 by Tachikawa and a few by Mansyu in Harbin, Manchuria. Though met in all parts of the Japanese war, the Ki-49 was not very effective; many were destroyed at Leyte Gulf, and by late 1944 all were being used either for non-combatant purposes or as suicide machines or, with ASV radar or magnetic-mine detectors, for ocean patrol. As it was a poor bomber three were converted as Ki-58 fighters with five 20mm cannon and three 12·7mm guns, while two were rebuilt as Ki-80 leadships for attack by fighter-bomber or suicide aircraft. The much more powerful III model was not ready by August 1945, though six were built.

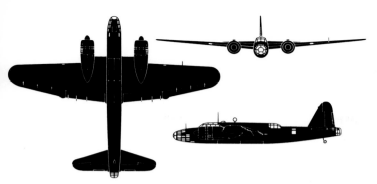

Above: Three-view of Ki-49-I (II has oil coolers under engines).

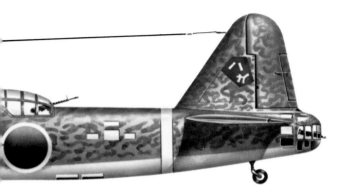

Above: The Ki-49-IIb was the main production version, and this example is typical. It was left in New Guinea but the unit to which it belonged has not been identified. The most probable colour scheme was a mottled light grey and olive green on the sides and upper surfaces and paler grey or sky underneath. No really good specimen of this important Army bomber exists today, though there are many wrecks.

Below: This excellent photograph shows a Ki-49-I in the home-based training role. It is probably finished in bright training orange overall, and carries on its tail stylised representations of the three Kanji characters spelling Hammamatsu, home of the Hammamatsu Army Bomber Training School. It is apparently not fitted with defensive armament.

North American NA-62 B-25 Mitchell

B-25 to TB-25N, PBJ series, F-10

Origin: North American Aviation Inc, Inglewood and Kansas City.

Type: Medium bomber and attack with crew from four to six (see text).

Engines: (B-25, A, B), two 1,700hp Wright R-2600-9 Double Cyclone 14-cylinder two-row radials; (C, D, G) two 1,700hp R-2600-13; (H, J, F-10), two 1,850hp (emergency rating) R-2600-29.

Dimensions: Span 67ft 7in (20·6m); length (B-25, A) 54ft 1in; (B, C, J) 52ft 11in (16·1m); (G, H) 51ft (15·54m); height (typical) 15ft 9in (4·80m).

Weights: Empty (J, typical) 21,100lb (9580kg); maximum loaded (A) 27,100lb; (B) 28,640lb; (C) 34,000lb (15,422kg); (G) 35,000lb (15,876kg); (H) 36,047lb (16,350kg); (J) normal 35,000lb, overload 41,800lb (18,960 kg).

Performance: Maximum speed (A) 315mph; (B) 300mph; (C, G) 284mph (459km/h); (H, J) 275mph (443km/h); initial climb (A, typical) 1,500ft (460m)/min; (late models, typical) 1,100ft (338m)/min; service ceiling (A) 27,000ft (8230m); (late models, typical) 24,000ft (7315m); range (all, typical) 1,500 miles (2414km).

Armament: See text.

History: First flight (NA-40 prototype) January 1939; (NA-62, the first production B-25) 19 August 1940; (B-25G) August 1942.

Users: (Wartime) Australia, Brazil, China, France (FFL), Italy (Co-Belligerent), Mexico, Netherlands (1944), Soviet Union, UK (RAF, RN), US (AAC/AAF, Navy).

Development: Named in honour of the fearless US Army Air Corps officer who was court-martialled in 1924 for his tiresome (to officialdom) belief in air power, the B-25 — designed by a company with no previous experience of twins, of bombers or of high performance warplanes — was made in larger quantities than any other American twin-engined combat ►

Below: One of the most heavily armed twin-engined aircraft of the war, this B-25J belonged to the 345th BG in the Philippines.

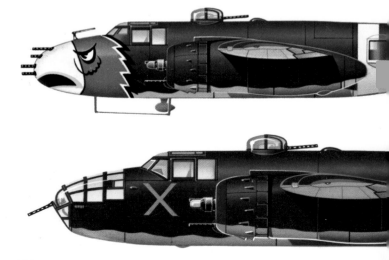

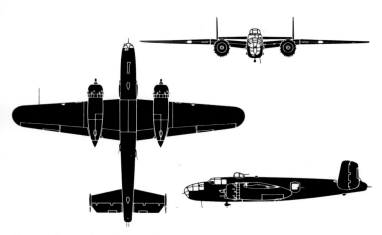

Above: Three-view of B-25J (RAF, Mitchell III).

Above: The bluff-nosed B-25G was the first model to carry a 75mm gun. This photograph was taken in the late summer of 1943.

Below: This Mitchell III (B-25J) served with an RAF Free French unit; serial number was KJ687.

Below: After World War II the B-25 Mitchell was popular with numerous air forces. This former B-25J (NA-240) spent more than 15 years with the Fuerza Aerea Uruguaya of Uruguay.

Below: After World War II the B-25 Mitchell was popular with numerous air forces. This former B-25J (NA-240) spent more than 15 years with the Fuerza Aerea Uruguaya of Uruguay.

aircraft and has often been described as the best aircraft in its class in World War II. Led by Lee Atwood and Ray Rice, the design team first created the Twin Wasp-powered NA-40, but had to start again and build a sleeker and more powerful machine to meet revised Army specifications demanding twice the bomb load (2,400lb, 1089kg). The Army ordered 184 off the drawing board, the first 24 being B-25s and the rest B-25A with armour and self-sealing tanks. The defensive armament was a 0·5in manually aimed in the cramped tail and single 0·3in manually aimed from waist windows and the nose; bomb load was 3,000lb (1361kg). The B had twin 0·5in in an electrically driven dorsal turret and a retractable ventral turret, the tail gun being removed. On 18 April 1942 16 B-25Bs led by Lt-Col Jimmy Doolittle made the daring and morale-raising raid on Tokyo,

having made free take-offs at gross weight from the carrier *Hornet* 800 miles distant. Extra fuel, external bomb racks and other additions led to the C, supplied to the RAF, China and Soviet Union, and as PBJ-1C to the US Navy. The D was similar but built at the new plant at Kansas City. In 1942 came the G, with solid nose fitted with a 75mm M-4 gun, loaded manually with 21 rounds. At first two 0·5in were also fixed in the nose, for flak suppression and sighting, but in July 1943 tests against Japanese ships showed that more was needed and the answer was four 0·5in "package guns" ▶

Below: Shadows race across the Tunisian desert as a squadron of USAAF B-25C Mitchells of the newly formed 12th Air Force head for a daytime target. Note RAF-style fin flashes.

Above: This B-25J was one of 870 of various sub-types supplied freely under Lend-Lease to the Soviet Union in 1941–44. The B-25 was supplied in greater numbers than any other Allied offensive aircraft, though the various A-20 versions ran it close.

Right: A dramatic photograph taken on 18 April 1942 as one of Lt-Col James H. Doolittle's B-25Cs staggers into the air from USS *Hornet* bound for Tokyo. The lead aircraft on this intrepid mission had a run of only 467 feet along the pitching deck.

on the sides of the nose. Next came the B-25H with the fearsome armament of a 75mm, 14 0·5in guns (eight firing ahead, two in waist bulges and four in dorsal and tail turrets) and a 2,000lb (907kg) torpedo or 3,200lb (1451kg) of bombs. Biggest production of all was of the J, with glazed nose, normal bomb load of 4,000lb (1814kg) and 13 0·5in guns supplied with 5,000 rounds. The corresponding attack version had a solid nose with five additional 0·5in guns. Total J output was 4,318, and the last delivery in August 1945 brought total output to 9,816. The F-10 was an unarmed multi-camera reconnaissance version, and the CB-25 was a post-war transport model. The wartime AT-24 trainers were redesignated TB-25 and, after 1947, supplemented by more than 900 bombers rebuilt as the TB-25J, K, L and M. Many ended their days as research hacks or target tugs and one carried the cameras for the early Cinerama films.

Petlyakov Pe-2 and Pe-3

Pe-2, 2I, 2R, 2U and 3bis

Origin: The design bureau of V. M. Petlyakov.
Type: (2) attack bomber; (2I) interceptor fighter; (2R) reconnaissance; (2U) dual trainer; (3bis) fighter reconnaissance.
Engines: Two Klimov (Hispano-Suiza basic design) vee-12 liquid-cooled; (2, pre-1943) 1,100hp M-105R or RA; (2, 1943 onwards, 2R, 2U, 3bis) 1,260hp M-105PF; (2I) 1,600hp M-107A.
Dimensions: Span 56ft 3½in (17·2m); length 41ft 4¼in to 41ft 6in (12·6–12·66m); height 11ft 6in (3·5m).
Weights: Empty (typical) 12.900lb (5870kg); normal loaded 16,540–16,976lb (7700kg); maximum loaded (all versions) 18,780lb (8520kg).
Performance: Maximum speed (typical, 105R) 336mph (540km/h); (105PF) 360mph (580km/h); (107A) 408mph (655km/h); initial climb (typical) 1,430ft (436m)/min; service ceiling (except 2I) 28,870ft (8800 m); (2I) 36,100ft (11,000m); range with bomb load (105R) 746 miles (1200km); (105PF) 721 miles (1160km).
Armament: See text.
History: First flight (VI-100) 1939; (production Pe-2) June 1940; final delivery, probably January 1945.
User: Soviet Union (post-war, Czechoslovakia, Poland).

Development: Not until long after World War II did Western observers appreciate the importance of the Pe-2. Built throughout the war, it was one of the outstanding combat aircraft of the Allies and, by dint of continual improvement, remained in the front rank of tactical fighting along the entire Eastern front right up to the German surrender. It was planned by Vladimir M. Petlyakov's design team in 1938 as a high-altitude fighter designated

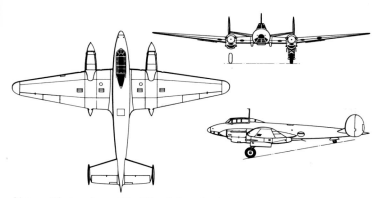

Above: Three-view of Pe-2 (basic bomber).

VI-100. When adapted to high-level bombing it kept the fighter's slim fuselage and this feature, coupled with intensive aerodynamic refinement, always made it fast enough to be difficult for German fighters to intercept it. Level bombing at height proved inaccurate, so dive brakes were added under the wings and the Pe-2 went into service in August 1940 as a multi-role dive and attack bomber, with crew of three and four 7·62mm ShKAS machine guns, two fixed firing ahead above the nose, one aimed from the upper rear position and one aimed from a retracting ventral mount with periscopic sight. Up to 2,205lb (1000kg) of bombs could be carried, either ▶

Below: Though it could not carry a 4,000lb bomb, as could some British Mosquitoes, the Pe-2 had a remarkably long weapon bay (with doors open in this picture) plus bays in the engine nacelles.

all externally or partly in the bomb bay and part in the rear of the long nacelles. The Pe-3bis fighter of 1941 had manoeuvre flaps instead of dive brakes, and additional fixed 20mm ShVAK and 12·7mm BS guns. During 1942 a 12·7mm power turret replaced the upper rear gun, the lower rear gun was made 12·7mm calibre and two 7·62mm beam guns were added. Extra armour, self-sealing tanks with cold exhaust-gas purging, detail drag-reduction and PF engines followed. The final versions had M-107 (VK-107) engines, various heavier armament and up to 6,615lb (3000kg) bomb load. Total production was just over 11,400.

From the basic three-seat low-level attack bomber, itself derived from a high-altitude fighter, stemmed numerous research or stillborn developments. One was the Pe-2VI high-altitude fighter, for which Dr M. N. Petrov's pressure cabin (planned for the original fighter) was resurrected. It had a heavy nose armament, but the high-flying threat (which was

Probably taken in 1943 this photo shows Pe-2FT bombers (FT stood for front-line request and added extra rear-firing guns and armour) which cruised so fast that escorting Hurricanes could not keep up!

expected to include the Ju 288) never materialised. One of the leaders on the VI team was Myasishchev, who later accomplished important designs in his own right. Another fighter version, about two years later in timing than the Pe-3bis, was the Pe-2I with direct-injection M-107A engines and a speed comfortably in excess of 400mph. Other versions included the Pe-2R long-range low- and high-level reconnaissance aircraft, with a large camera installation instead of a bomb bay, and the Pe-2UT trainer with tandem dual controls. In 1943–45 a Pe-2R was also used for ground and flight rocket tests by the RD-1 nitric acid/kerosene engine, installed in the tail; 169 firings were made.

Petlyakov Pe-8

ANT-42, TB-7, Pe-8 (various sub-types)

Origin: The design bureau of A. N. Tupolev, with team headed by V. M. Petlyakov.

Type: Heavy bomber with normal crew of nine.

Engines: (Prototype) see text; (first production) four 1,300hp Mikulin AM-35A vee-12 liquid-cooled; (second production) four 1,475hp Charomski M-30B vee-12 diesels; (third production) four 1,630hp Shvetsov ASh-82FNV 14-cylinder two-row radials.

Dimensions: Span 131ft 0½in (39·94m); length 73ft 8¾in (22·47m); height 20ft (6·1m).

Weights: Empty (first production) 37,480lb (17,000kg); (typical late production) about 40,000lb (18,000kg); maximum loaded (early) 63,052lb (28,600kg); (late, M-30B) 73,469lb (33,325kg); (ASh-82) 68,519lb (31,080kg).

Performance: Maximum speed (AM-35) 276mph (444km/h); (M-30B) 272mph (438km/h); (ASh-82) 280mph (451km/h); initial climb (typical) 853ft (260m)/min; service ceiling (AM-35, M-30B) about 22,966ft (7000m); (ASh-82) 29,035ft (8850m); range, see text.

Armament: (Typical) one 20mm ShVAK in dorsal and tail turrets, two 7·62mm ShKAS in nose turret and one 12·7mm BS manually aimed from rear of each inner nacelle; bomb load, see text.

History: First flight (ANT-42) 27 December 1936; (production TB-7) early 1939; (ASh-82 version) 1943; final delivery 1944.

User: Soviet Union (ADD).

Development: Despite the Soviet Union's great heritage of impressive heavy bombers the TB-7 was the only aircraft in this category in World War II and only a few hundred were built. This resulted from a Germanic concentration on twin-engined tactical machines rather than any short-coming in the Pe-8 and there was at no time any serious problem with propulsion, though the type of engine kept changing. The prototype, built

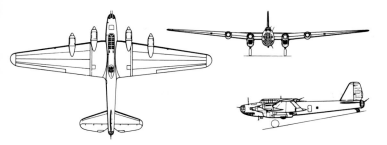

Above: Three-view of Pe-8 first series with AM-35 engines.

to a 1934 specification, had four 1,100hp M-105 engines supercharged by a large blower driven by an M-100 engine in the rear fuselage. Another had AM-34FRN engines, but the AM-35A was chosen for production at Kuznets in 1939, by which time the complex ACN-2 supercharging system had been abandoned. Performance at 8000m (26,250ft, double the maximum-speed height for earlier Soviet heavies) was outstanding and faster than the Bf 109B. In 1940, in line with the new Soviet designation system, the TB-7 was credited to Petlyakov, leader of the design team. Unfortunately he was killed in a crash two years later and most of the wartime development was managed by I. F. Nyezeval. Maximum bomb load was 8,818lb (4000kg), the range of 2,321 miles being raised to over 3,000 miles by the diesel engines substituted when AM-35 production ceased. The final radial-engined version could carry 11,600lb for 2,500 miles and many long missions were made into Hungary, Romania and East Germany the first major mission being on Berlin in mid-1941.

Below: The final Nyezeval-managed variant had direct-injection Ash-82FNV engines with slim inner nacelles, but not many were built owing to concentration on tactical bombers. The 4,410lb (2000kg) bomb was carried internally – but not very often.

PZL P.23 and 43 Karaś

P.23A and B, P.43A and B

Origin: Panstwowe Zaklady Lotnicze, Poland.
Type: Three-seat reconnaissance bomber.
Engine: (P.23A) one 580hp PZL (Bristol-licence) Pegasus II nine-cylinder radial; (P.23B) 680hp PZL Pegasus VIII; P.43A, 930hp Gnome-Rhône 14 Kfs 14-cylinder two-row radial; (P.43B) 980hp G-R 14N1.
Dimensions: Span 45ft 9in (13·95m); length (23) 31ft 9in (9·68m); (43) 32ft 10in; height 11ft 6in (3·5m).
Weights: Empty (23, typical) 4,250lb (1928kg); loaded (23) 6,918lb (3138kg); maximum overload 7,774lb (3526kg).
Performance: Maximum speed (23A) 198mph (320km/h); (23B) 217mph (350km/h); (43B) 227mph (365km/h); initial climb (typical) 985ft (300m)/min; service ceiling (typical) 24,600ft (7500m); range with bomb load, 410 miles (660km) (overload, 932 miles, 1500km).
Armament: (23) one 7·7mm Browning or KM Wz 33 firing forward, one on PZL hydraulically assisted mount in rear cockpit and third similarly mounted in rear ventral position; external bomb load of up to 1,543lb (700kg); (43) as 23 but with two forward-firing guns, one on each side of cowling.
History: First flight (P.23/I) August 1934; (production Karaś A) June 1936; (P.43A) 1937.
Users: Bulgaria, Poland, Romania.

Development: Designed by a team led by Stanisław Prauss, the P.23 was hardly beautiful yet it provided the tactical attack capability of one of Europe's largest air forces in the late 1930s. By the outbreak of World War II, 14 of the bomber regiments of the Polish Air Force had been equipped with the Karaś (Carp); its successor, the greatly improved Sum, was about to enter service. When designed, in 1931—32, the Karaś was an outstandingly

Below: The Karaś entered service in late 1936 and eventually equipped 14 squadrons, at least two of which are seen in this 1938 photograph on parade for inspection. When the Germans invaded Poland in 1939 the type equipped 12 squadrons, seven of them attached to the land armies and five forming the independent Bomber Brigade. During the desperate four-week campaign they were flown with great gallantry though they suffered severe losses.

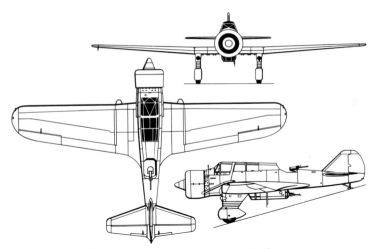

Above: Three-view of P.23A (P.23B almost identical).

modern aircraft, one of its radical features being the use of smooth skin of light-alloy/balsa sandwich construction. It carried a bomb load far heavier than any of its contemporaries and had no defence "blind spots", though its firepower was meagre. The more powerful P.43 was built for Bulgaria, 12 43A being followed by an order for 42 of the B model of which nearly all were delivered by the start of World War II. Despite skill and heroism the Polish squadrons were soon overwhelmed, but a handful of Karaś managed to reach Romania, where they were refurbished, put into service with Romanian crews and used on the Bessarabian front in the invasion of the Soviet Union in 1941.

Below: The national eagle on a pentagon badge shows that this Karaś B served with the same regiment as the aircraft in the foreground opposite; all regiments displayed their badges in this position, except for Karaś A aircraft at training schools. Colour was dark olive green with pale grey underside. The P.23 Karaś was an outstandingly fine attack bomber when it first flew in the mid-1930s, but it was obsolescent by 1939 and was an easy prey for German fighters.

PZL P.37 Łoś

P.37-I Łoś A and P.37-II Łoś B (Łoś = Elk).

Origin: Panstwowe Zaklady Lotnicze, Poland.
Type: Medium bomber.
Engines: Two PZL-built Bristol Pegasus nine-cylinder radials, (Łoś A) 875hp Pegasus XIIB, (B) 925hp Pegasus XX.
Dimensions: Span 58ft 8¾in (17·90m); length 42ft 4in (12·90m); height 16ft 8in (5·08m).
Weights: Empty 9,293lb (4213kg); normal loaded 18,739lb (8500kg); max overload 19,577lb (8880kg).
Performance: Maximum speed 273mph (440km/h); service ceiling 19,685ft (6000m); range with 3,880lb (1760kg) bomb load 1,616 miles (2600km).
Armament: Single manually aimed 7·7mm KM Wz.37 machine guns in nose, dorsal and ventral positions; internal (fuselage and wing) bays for bomb load of up to 5,688lb (2580kg).
History: First flight June 1936; service delivery, spring 1938.
Users: Poland, Romania.

Development: Designed by a team led by Jerzy Dabrowski in 1934, this bomber (extraordinarily efficient in its ratio of empty to gross weight) was the subject of unwarranted political criticism instigated by the Army ground forces. Nevertheless by the outbreak of war four squadrons, with nine Łoś B each, were operational with the Bomber Brigade and they proved extremely effective in the few days they were able to operate. About 100 had been delivered, and a dozen more were readied for combat during the Polish campaign, some 40 Łoś A and B finally escaping to Romania. There they were taken over and in 1941 used against the Soviet Union, a few still serving as target tugs in the late 1950s. By 1938 the dramatic performance of the Łoś resulted in intense international interest, and had war not supervened PZL would have fulfilled export contracts for at least five, and probably nine, countries.

Below: Air and ground crews parade with their Los A bombers at the IIIrd Dyon (Conversion Unit) in late 1938.

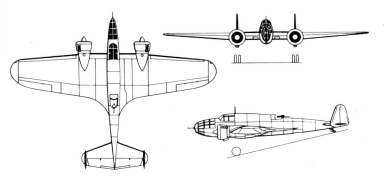

Above: Three-view of P.37 Łoś A (Łoś B outwardly identical).

Below: One of the first Łoś B bombers, pictured with a regiment of P.11c fighters shortly before the German attack on 1 September 1939. The P.37 Łoś was possibly the best bomber in the world in service at that time, yet it was unwanted by the Army chiefs who sought by every means possible to stop production and disrupt training. Despite this the Bomber Brigade had managed to form four Dyons (each equivalent to a squadron), Nos 211, 212, 216 and 217, with nine aircraft each, and complete initial training.

Savoia-Marchetti S.M.79 Sparviero

S.M.79-I, II and III, 79B and 79-JR

Origin: SIAI "Savoia-Marchetti"; built under licence (79-II) by Aeronautica Macchi and OM "Reggiane"; (79 JR) Industria Aeronautica Romana.
Type: 4/5-seat bomber, torpedo bomber and reconnaissance.
Engines: (I) three 780hp Alfa-Romeo 126 RC34 nine-cylinder radials; (II) three 1,000hp Piaggio P.XI RC40 14-cylinder two-row radials (one batch, 1,030hp Fiat A.80 RC41); (79B) two engines (many types); (79-JR) two 1,220hp Junker Jumo 211Da inverted-vee-12 liquid-cooled.
Dimensions: Span 69ft 6½in (21·2m); length (I) 51ft 10in; (II) 53ft 1¾in (16·2m); (B -JR) 52ft 9in; height'(II) 13ft 5½in (4·1m)   *continued* ▶

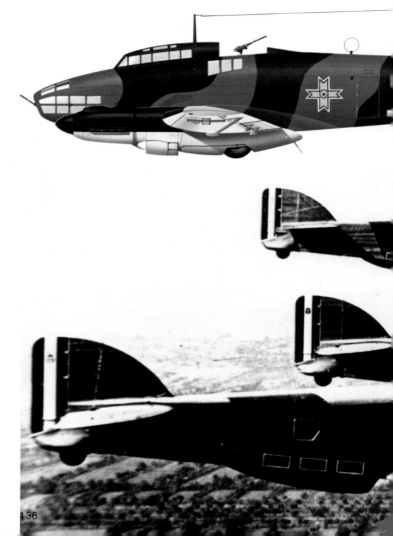

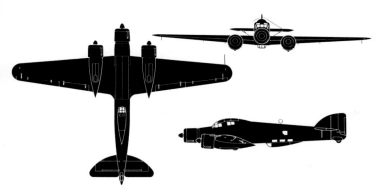

Above: Three-view of a typical S.M. 79-II.

Left: In appearance and character quite unlike the familiar tri-motor bomber of the Regia Aeronautica, the S.M.79-JR of the Royal Air Forces of Romania was powered by the same engines as a Heinkel 111H, two Jumo 211 liquid-cooled units. This example served with the 3rd Air Corps on the Eastern front in 1943, by which time it was operating mainly by night.

Below: Early S.M.79-I bombers of the Regia Aeronautica's 52° Squadriglia, photographed shortly before Italy entered the war in 1940. The upper surface colours were dark green and khaki.

Weights: Empty (I) 14,990lb (6800kg); (II) 16,755lb (7600kg); (-JR) 15,860lb (7195kg); maximum loaded (I) 23,100lb (10,500kg); (II) 24,192lb (11,300kg); (-JR) 23,788lb (10,470kg).

Performance: Maximum speed (I) 267mph; (II) 270mph (434km/h); (B) 255mph; (-JR) 276mph; initial climb (typical) 1,150ft (350m)/min; service ceiling (all) 21,325–23,300ft (7000m); range with bomb load (not torpedoes), typical, 1,243 miles (2000km).

Armament: (Typical) one 12·7mm Breda-SAFAT fixed firing ahead from above cockpit, one 12·7mm manually aimed from open dorsal position, one 12·7mm manually aimed from rear of ventral gondola and one 7·7mm Lewis manually aimed from either beam window; internal bomb bay for up to 2,200lb (1000kg) or two 450mm torpedoes slung externally; (79B and -JR) no fixed gun, typically three/five 7·7mm guns and bomb load up to 2,640lb (1200kg).

History: First flight (civil prototype) late 1934; service delivery (I) late 1936; (II) October 1939; final delivery (III) early 1944.

Users: Brazil, Iraq, Italy (RA, CB, ARSI), Jugoslavia, Romania, Spain (Nationalist).

Development: Though often derided — as were most Italian arms in World War II — the S.M.79 Sparviero (Hawk) was a fine and robust bomber that unfailingly operated in the most difficult conditions with great reliability. The prototype, fitted with various engines and painted in civil (or military) liveries, set various world records in 1935–36, despite its mixed structure of steel tube, light alloy, wood and fabric. Built at unprecedented rate for the Regia Aeronautica, the 79-I established an excellent reputation with

The final production version of the Sparviero was the S.M.79-III, which had no ventral gondola and also defended the pilot even better than earlier models by changing the cockpit-roof gun for a 20mm cannon. This picture shows a twin-finned Cant Z.1007bis on the left and two German gliders, a DFS 230 and Go 242, on the right, probably in early 1943.

Above: A rare colour photograph of S.M.79-II torpedo bombers of the famous and courageous Squadriglie Aerosiluranti.

the Aviación Legionaria in the Spanish civil war, while other Stormi laid the basis for great proficiency with torpedoes. Altogether about 1,200 of all versions served with the Regia Aeronautica, while just over 100 were exported. Most exports were twin-engined 79B versions, but the Romanian-built 79-JR was more powerful and served on the Russian front in 1941–44.

Savoia-Marchetti S.M.81 Pipistrello

S.M.81 Pipistrello (Bat) of many serie

Origin: SIAI "Savoia-Marchetti".
Type: Multi-role bomber, transport and utility.
Engines: (Most) three aircooled radials, usually 700hp Piaggio P.X nine-cylinder; others 580hp Alfa Romeo 125, 680hp Piaggio P.IX, 900hp Alfa Romeo 126 and 1,000hp Gnome-Rhône K-14; (81B, two engines, various).
Dimensions: Span 78ft 8¾in (24·00m); length (typical) 58ft 4¾in (17·80 m); height 14ft 7¼in (4·45m).
Weights: Empty (typical) 13,890lb (6300kg); max loaded 23,040lb (10,450kg).
Performance: Maximum speed 211mph (340km/h); typical range with bomb load 932 miles (1500km).
Armament: Varied or absent, but usually two 7·7mm Breda-SAFAT in powered dorsal turret, two more in retractable ventral turret and two more aimed manually from beam windows; internal weapon bay for up to 2,205lb (1000kg) of bombs.
History: First flight 1935; service delivery, autumn 1935; final delivery, possibly 1941.
Users: Italy (RA, CB, ARSI, post-war AF), Spain.

SNCASE LeO 451

LeO 45, 451 B4 and derivatives

Origin: Soc Lioré et Olivier, Argenteuil, in 1937 nationalized as part of SNCASE; production see text.
Type: Medium bomber, later transport.
Engines: Two 1,140hp Gnome-Rhône 14N 48/49 14-cylinder radials.
Dimensions: Span 73ft 10¾in (22·52m); length 56ft 4in (17·17m); height 14ft 9¼in (4·50m).
Weights: Empty 17,225lb (7813kg); normal loaded 25,133lb (11,400kg); max 26,455lb (12,000kg).
Performance: Maximum speed 307mph (495km/h); service ceiling 29,530ft (9000m); range with 1,102lb (500kg) bomb load 1,430 miles (2300km).
Armament: One 20mm Hispano-Suiza 404 cannon in SAMM retractable dorsal turret, 7·5mm MAC 1934 in retractable ventral turret and MAC 1934 fixed in nose firing ahead; internal bay for up to 4,410lb (2000kg) of bombs.
History: First flight 16 January 1937; service delivery 16 August 1939; final delivery 1943.
Users: France (Armée de l'Air, Vichy French and post-war AF), Germany (Luftwaffe), Italy (RA and CB), UK (RAF) and US (AAF).

Development: Beyond doubt the best bomber developed in France in the final years before the war, the LeO 45 was also available in substantial numbers. Despite chaotic conditions caused by nationalization of the air-frame industry and widespread sabotage, production at Paris (Clichy and Levallois) and assembly at Villacoublay got into its stride by the spring of 1939. To provide the stipulated catwalk past the bomb bay small secondary bays were added in the inner wing and the main bay made even narrower than the slim fuselage. Production was dispersed to take in factories

Above: Most of the large force of S.M.81 bomber/transports prior to World War II were silver or cream, but this example was one of many whose wing upper surfaces were banded with red.

Development: A military version of the very successful S.M.73 airliner, the S.M.81 was one of the world's best multi-role bomber/transport aircraft in 1935, but when Italy entered World War II in June 1940 (by which time about 100 were in service, plus about 40 in Spain) it was becoming obsolescent. Despite this its serviceability and popularity resulted in it appearing in every theatre in which Italy was engaged, from Eritrea to the Soviet Union. Until 1942 it was an important night bomber in the eastern Mediterranean, and it became the most important Italian transport in terms of numbers (though much inferior to the S.M.82 in capability). A few served with the post-war Aeronautica Militare until about 1951.

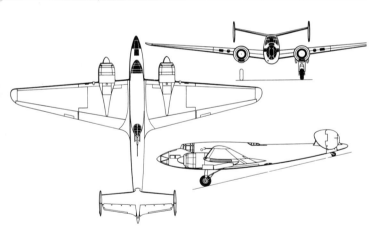

Above: Three-view of LeO 451 B4 with armament retracted.

around Lyons, a second assembly-line at Ambérieu (Ain) and a third line at Marignane (Marseilles), and the evacuated Villacoublay plant was hastily moved to an underground works at Cravant near Auxerre in May 1940. The 451 B4 had been in action from the first day of war, and by May 1940 some 472 equipped eight Armée de l'Air groups. Missions could not have been more impossible, negating all the type's brilliant qualities, 47 being lost in the first 288 sorties (though on one mission the dorsal gunner destroyed two Bf 110s). Several sub-types served the Vichy forces and Luftwaffe, one Gruppe switching from Stalingrad to equip with the LeO 451T. Italy, the RAF and USAAF used the aircraft chiefly as a utility transport.

Short S.29 Stirling

Stirling I to V

Origin: Short Brothers, Rochester and Belfast.
Type: (I–III) heavy bomber with crew of 7/8; (IV) glider tug and special transport; (V) strategic transport.
Engines: (I) four 1,595hp Bristol Hercules XI 14-cylinder sleeve-valve radials; (II) 1,600hp Wright R-2600-A5B Cyclone; (III, IV, V) 1,650hp Bristol Hercules XVI.
Dimensions: Span 99ft 1in (30·2m); length (except V) 87ft 3in (26·6m); (V) 90ft 6¾in (27·6m); height 22ft 9in (6·94m).
Weights: Empty (I) 44,000lb (19,950kg); (III) 46,900lb (21,273kg); (IV, V, typical) 43,200lb (19,600kg); maximum loaded (I) 59,400lb (26,943kg); (III, IV, V) 70,000lb (31,750kg).
Performance: Maximum speed (I–III) 270mph (435km/h); (IV, V) 280mph (451km/h); initial climb (typical) 800ft (244m)/min; service ceiling (I–III) 17,000ft (5182m); range (III) 590 miles (950km) with 14,000lb bombs or 2,010 miles (3235km) with 3,500lb; range (IV, V) 3,000 miles (4828km).
Armament: (I) two 0·303in Brownings in nose and dorsal turrets and four in tail turret, plus (early batches) two in remote control ventral turret; ▶

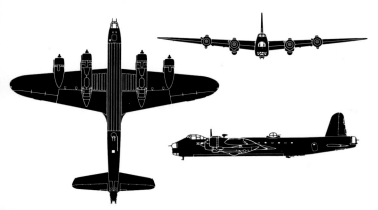

Above: Three-view of Stirling I with FN.64 ventral turret.

Below: One of an outstanding series of colour photographs taken in 1941 on a visit to 149 Sqn, one of the first Stirling users. At this time the RAF was still trying to make deep penetrations of the Continent in daylight —not a good idea with Stirlings.

maximum bomb load 18,000lb (8165kg) in fuselage and inner wings; (II, III) as (I) but different dorsal turret; (IV) sole armament, tail turret; (V) none.

History: First flight 14 May 1939; (production Mk I) May 1940; final delivery (V) November 1945.

User: UK (RAF).

Development: Though extremely impressive, with vast length, unprecedented height and even two separate tailwheels, the Stirling was unpopular. Partly owing to short wing span it had a poor ceiling and sluggish manoeuvrability except at low level. Though it carried a heavy bomb load,

Below: This Stirling I is of the intermediate series of 1941 between the first Series I (no dorsal turret) and the Mk I Series III with the Lancaster-type dorsal turret as also fitted to the Mk III. This Series II had the unpopular F.N.7-mod dorsal turret similar to that of the Botha and Manchester I.

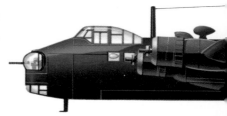

it could not carry bombs bigger than 2,000lb (the largest size when the design was completed in 1938). Operations began with daylight attacks in February 1941, soon switched to night, and by 1943 the Stirling was regarded mainly as a tug and transport and carrier of ECM jamming and spoofing devices for 100 Group. The RAF received 2,221 bomber versions, excluding the two Mk II conversions, and Short's new Belfast plant finally built 160 of the streamlined Mk V transports which carried 40 troops or heavy freight.

Below: A late-production Stirling I Series III with definitive dorsal turret, serving with 214 Sqn based at Stradishall in late 1942.

Tupolev SB-2

ANT-40, SB-1, -2 and -2bis (ANT-41)

Origin: The design bureau of A. N. Tupolev.

Type: Medium bomber with usual crew of three.

Engines: Two vee-12 liquid-cooled; (early -2 versions) 750hp VK-100 (M-100) derived from Hispano-Suiza 12Y; (late -2 versions) 840hp M-100A; (-2bis versions) 1,100hp M-103.

Dimensions: Span 66ft 8½in (20·34m); length (with very few exceptions) 40ft 3¼in (12·29m); height 10ft 8in (3·28m).

Weights: Empty (early -2) 8,267lb (3750kg); (M-100A) typically 8,820lb (4000kg); (-2bis) about 10,800lb (4900kg); maximum loaded (early -2) 13,449lb (6100kg); (M-100A) 13,955lb (6330kg), (-2bis) normally 17,196lb (7800kg); overload 21,165lb (9600kg).

Performance: Maximum speed (early) 255mph (410km/h); (M-100A) 263mph (425km/h); (-2bis) 280mph (450km/h); initial climb (-2bis) 1,310ft (400m)/min; service ceiling (typical later version) 31,000—35,000ft (9500—10,500m); range with bomb load (typical -2) 746 miles (1200km); (-2bis, max fuel) 994 miles (1600km).

Armament: (Normal for all versions) four 7·62mm ShKAS machine guns, two manually aimed through vertical slits in nose, one from dorsal position and one from rear ventral position; internal bomb bay for six 220lb (100kg) or single 1,100lb (500kg).

History: First flight (SB-1) 7 October 1934; service delivery (-2) early 1936; (-2bis) probably late 1938; final delivery, probably 1942.

Users: China, Soviet Union, Spain (Republican).

Below: When it entered service in January 1936 the SB-2 outperformed every other bomber. This was one of more than 200 supplied to the Republican forces in Spain (Grupo de Bombardeo 24).

Right: This SB-2, again one of the 1936-37 vintage with flat-fronted radiators but in this case fitted with propeller spinners, was one of a considerable number supplied to the Chinese Central Government in early 1938. It formed the core of Chinese bomber strength.

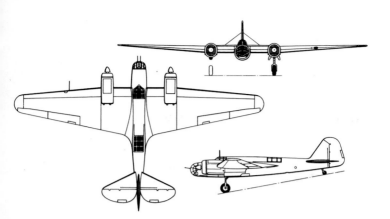

Above: Three-view of early SB-2 as used from 1936.

Development: Like the TB-3, the SB-2 was built in great numbers in the 1930s and bore a heavy burden in "the Great Patriotic War" from June 1941 until long after it was obsolescent. Though built to a 1933 specification it was actually much superior to Britain's later Blenheim and it was the Soviet Union's first stressed-skin bomber. The SB-1 prototype had M-25 radials, but performance was even better with the VK-100 in-lines and service in the Spanish civil war in 1936–39 initially found the Nationalists lacking any fighters able to catch the speedy, high-flying SB. In speed and rate of ▶

Left: Though retaining the same basic airframe as earlier versions, with local reinforcement for increased weights and speeds, this SB-2bis was one of the later series (bis suffix) with streamlined cowlings incorporating ducted radiators. A dorsal turret was added and the rear ventral position was improved. The aircraft depicted was wrecked at Lvov in the first days of the German invasion.

climb even the first service versions surpassed contemporary fighters and, despite a considerable increase in fuel capacity and weight, performance was improved with the more streamlined M-103, without the original bluff frontal radiators. Total production exceeded 6,000 of all versions, and the type served against Japan in 1938–39, in Finland and against German forces until 1943, the last two years mainly in the role of a night bomber.

Tupolev TB-3
ANT-6, TB-3 Types 1932, 1934 and 1936

Origin: The design bureau of A. N. Tupolev.
Type: Heavy bomber with crew of ten (Type 1932) and later six.
Engines: Four vee-12 liquid-cooled; (1932) 730hp M-17; (1934) 900hp M-34R (derived from BMW VI); later 950–1,280hp M-34RN or RNF.
Dimensions: Span 132ft 10½in (40·5m); (1936) 137ft 1½in (41·8m); length (early) 81ft (24·69m); (1934 onward) 82ft 8¼in (25·21m); height, not available but about 18ft.
Weights: Empty, 22,000–26,450lb (11,000–12,000kg); maximum loaded (1932) 38,360lb (17,500kg); (1934) 41,021lb (18,606kg); (1936) 41,226lb (18,700kg), with overload of 54,020lb (24,500kg).
Performance: Maximum speed (M-17, 1932) 134mph (215km/h); (M-34R, 1934) 144mph (232km/h); (M-34RN, 1936) 179mph (288km/h); initial climb, not available; service ceiling (1932) 12,467ft (3800m); (1934) 15,090ft (4600m); (1936) 25,365ft (7750m); range with bomb load (typical of all) 1,550 miles (2500km).
Armament: (1932, 1934) five pairs of 7·62mm DA-2 machine guns in nose, two dorsal mountings and two underwing positions, all manually aimed; internal bomb cells for maximum load of 4,850lb (2200kg); (1936) five (later three or four) 7·62mm ShKAS manually aimed, by 1936 without wing positions; bomb load up to 12,790lb (5800kg) carried on 26 fuselage racks and 12 external racks under fuselage and wings.
History: First flight (ANT-6) 22 December 1930; (production TB-3) probably late 1931; (M-34 prototype) March 1933; final delivery, probably 1939.
Users: China, Soviet Union.

Development: Though seemingly archaic in appearance — and its basic design dated from 1926 — the TB-3 was a large and formidable aircraft with capabilities outstripping those of any other bomber in service in other

Above: In the first week following the German invasion of the Soviet Union on 22 June 1941 more than two-thirds of Russian aircraft were destroyed, mostly on the ground. Here a surviving SB-2 of the early series is pushed into a wood for cover. Once a world-beater, Tupolev's speedy tactical bomber had by this time become obsolescent, though still extremely useful.

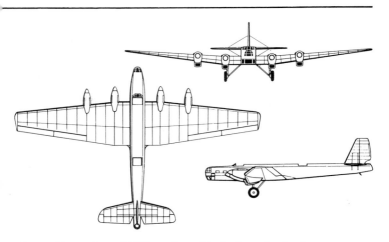

Above: Three-view of 1936 version with single mainwheels.

countries. Though not a stressed-skin design it was a cantilever monoplane with corrugated metal skin using Junkers technology and, thanks to generous stressing, had a considerable "stretching" capability that was put to good use during its long career. A leader in the Tupolev design team was young V. M. Petlyakov, later to produce bombers in his own right, but the aircraft was always known by its functional designation. The 1934 version had brakes on the tandem wire-spoked wheels, a tail turret in place of the underwing positions, and geared engines, which in 1935 were super-charged RN type. Altogether at least 800 of these fine machines were built, final models having smooth skin, single-wheel main gears and only three gunners in enclosed manual turrets. TB-3s saw much action against Japan, Poland, Finland and the German invader and served until 1944 as freight and paratroop transports.

Tupolev Tu-2

ANT-58, Tu-2 (many sub-variants), Tu-6

Origin: The design bureau of A. N. Tupolev.
Type: Attack bomber with normal crew of four.
Engines: Two 1,850hp Shvetsov ASh-82FN or FNV 14-cylinder two-row radials.
Dimensions: Span 61ft 10½in (18·86m); length 45ft 3¾in (13·8m); height 13ft 9½in (4·20m).
Weights: Empty 18,240lb (8273kg); maximum loaded 28,219lb (12,800kg).
Performance: Maximum speed 342mph (550km/h); initial climb 2,300ft (700m)/min;' service ceiling 31,168ft (9500m); range with 3,307lb (1500kg) bombs 1,553 miles (2500km).
Armament: Typically three manually aimed 12·7mm Beresin BS, one in upper rear of crew compartment, one in rear dorsal position and one in rear ventral position, and two 20mm ShVAK, each with 200 rounds, fixed in wing roots for ground attack (later, often 23mm); internal bomb bay for maximum load of 5,000lb (2270kg), later 6,615lb (3000kg).
History: First flight (ANT-58) October 1940; (production Tu-2) August 1942; final delivery 1948.
User: (Wartime) Soviet Union.

Development: Though it was undoubtedly one of the outstanding designs of World War II, the Tu-2 had the misfortune to emerge into a Soviet Union teeming with the Pe-2, and the older and smaller machine continued to be

Below: In 1950 about 200 Tu-2s were supplied to the newly formed People's Republic of China air force. This example is from the batch with three rear windows on each side.

Below: Numerous Tu-2s were supplied in the immediate post-war era to satellite air forces; this aircraft served with Poland.

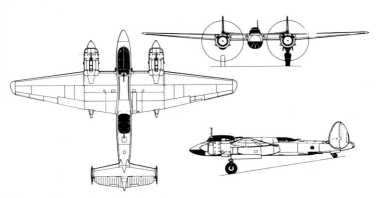

Above; Three-view of typical Tu-2.

produced at just ten times the rate of its supposed replacement (much the same happened with German bombers). It was formidable and reliable in service, extremely popular and hardly needed any major modification in the course of a career which extended right through the nervous Berlin Airlift (1948), Korea (1950–53, in North Korean service) and up to 1961 with several Communist nations. Known to NATO as "Bat", the post-war variants included a close-support type with 37mm cannon, a radar-equipped (night fighter?) variant and the high-altitude Tu-6 with long span and bigger tail.

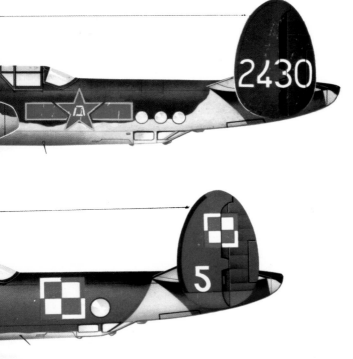

Vickers Wellesley

Type 287, Wellesley I and II

Origin: Vickers (Aviation) Ltd.
Type: Two-seat general-purpose bomber.
Engine: One 925hp Bristol Pegasus XX nine-cylinder radial.
Dimensions: Span 74ft 7in (22·73m); length 39ft 3in (11·96m); height 12ft 4in (3·75m).
Weights: Empty 6,369lb (2889kg); maximum loaded (except record flight) 11,100lb (5035kg).
Performance: Maximum speed 228mph (369km/h); initial climb 1,200ft (366m)/min; service ceiling 33,000ft (10,060m); range with bomb load 1,110 miles (1786km).
Armament: One 0·303in belt-fed Vickers in right wing firing ahead, one Vickers K manually aimed from rear cockpit; four 500lb (227kg) or eight 250lb bombs in streamlined containers, originally fitted with bomb doors, under wings.

History: First flight 19 June 1935; service delivery April 1937; final delivery May 1938.
User: UK (RAF), possibly passed on to other Middle East countries.

Development: Vickers built a large biplane to meet the RAF G.4/31 specification, but it was so humdrum the company board decided at their own risk to build a monoplane using the radical geodetic (metal basketwork) construction developed for airships by their structural wizard B.N. (later Sir Barnes) Wallis. The result was so dramatically superior the Air Ministry lost its fear of monoplanes and bought 176 as the Wellesley. Distinguished by great span, high aspect ratio, extreme cruise efficiency and a most reliable engine (identical in size to the Jupiter but of virtually twice the power) it was natural to form a special Long-Range Development Flight. Three aircraft, with three seats, extra fuel and long-chord cowlings, took off from Ismailia, Egypt, on 5 November 1938; one landed at Koepang and the other two reached Darwin, 7,162 miles (11,525km) in 48 hours non-stop. In World War II Wellesleys were extremely active in East Africa, Egypt, the Middle East and surrounding sea areas until late 1942.

Left: One of the very first Wellesleys to reach the RAf was this example delivered to 76 Sqn at RAF Finningley, Yorkshire, in April 1937.

Below: The Wellesley saw most of its service in east and north-east Africa in 1940-42. This example, pictured in 1940, has the hood of the rear cockpit swung open and the gun ready for action. The containers housed the bombs.

Vickers-Armstrongs Wellington
Type 415 and 440, Wellington I to T.19

Origin: Vickers-Armstrongs (Aircraft) Ltd.

Type: Originally long-range bomber with crew of six; later, see text.

Engines: Variously two Bristol Pegasus nine-cylinder radials, two Rolls-Royce Merlin vee-12 liquid-cooled, two Pratt & Whitney Twin Wasp 14-cylinder two-row radials or two Bristol Hercules 14-cylinder two-row sleeve-valve radials; for details see text.

Dimensions: Span 86ft 2in (26·26m); (V, VI) 98ft 2in; length (most) 64ft 7in (19·68m), (some, 60ft 10in or, with Leigh light, 66ft); height 17ft 6in (5·33m), (some 17ft).

Weights: Empty (IC) 18,556lb (8417kg); (X) 26,325lb (11,940kg); maximum loaded (IC) 25,800lb (11,703kg); (III) 29,500lb (13,381kg); (X) 36,500lb (16,556kg).

Performance: Maximum speed (IC) 235mph (379km/h); (most other marks) 247–256mph (410km/h); (V, VI) 300mph (483km/h); initial climb (all, typical) 1,050ft (320m)/min; service ceiling (bomber versions, typical) 22,000ft (6710m); (V, VI) 38,000ft (11,600m); range with weapon load of 1,500lb (680kg), typically 2,200 miles (3540km).

Armament: See text.

History: First flight (B.9/32) 15 June 1936; (production Mk I) 23 December 1937; service delivery (I) October 1938; final delivery (T.10) 13 October 1945.

Users: (Wartime) Australia, Czechoslovakia, France, New Zealand, Poland, UK (RAF).

Development: It was natural that Vickers (Aviation), from October 1938 Vickers-Armstrongs (Aicraft), should have followed up the success of the Wellesley with a larger bomber using the geodetic form of construction. There were difficulties in applying it to wings, cut-out nacelles and fuselages with large bomb-doors and turrets, but the B.9/32 prototype was obviously efficient, and by September 1939 had been developed into Britain's most formidable bomber. The following were chief versions:

I Powered by 1,050hp Pegasus XVIII and originally with twin 0·303in Brownings in simple Vickers turrets at nose and tail; internal bomb load 4,500lb (2041kg). Built one-a-day at Weybridge, later a further 50 per month at Chester and, later still, about 30 a month at Squire's Gate, Blackpool. Mk IA had Nash and Thompson power turrets, and the main IC version had two beam guns (some earlier had a ventral barbette). Production: 180+ 183+ 2,685.

II Had 1,145hp Merlin X, otherwise as IC. Production: 400.

III Main Bomber Command type in 1941–2, with 1,375hp Hercules III or XI, and four-gun tail turret. Production: 1,519.

IV Flown by two Polish squadrons, powered by 1,200hp Twin Wasp R-1830-S3C4-G. Production: 220.

continued ▶

Right: One of the 2,685 Wellington IC bombers, in this case from the Shadow Factory at Chester. It is depicted as it was in 1940, serving with 150 Sqn at Newton, near Nottingham. All later bomber versions had greater power and increased armament.

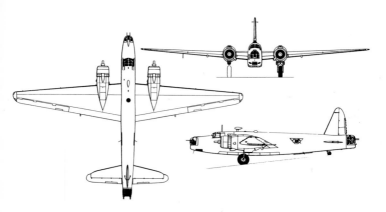

Above: Three-view of Wellington III (other Hercules versions similar).

Above: Although the colour has faded with age, this is an original photograph dating from 1940–41, showing 20 bombs of nominal 250lb size going aboard a Wellington IC. At the time, this was the RAF's most formidable bomber, but bigger ones were in prospect.

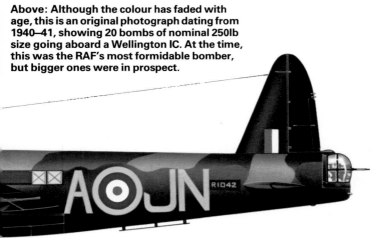

Above: Wellington I series 1 bombers of the only two squadrons then equipped with the new bomber (9 and 149) took part in air exercises in summer 1939. This early model had four machine guns in "roll-top desk" fairings at nose and tail.

Below: One of the first batch of 200 Merlin-engined Wellington IIs, of which 585 were built in all (all at Weybridge). This photograph was taken in 1941, by which time the new standard mark was the Hercules-engined III with four-gun rear turret.

V Experimental pressurised high-altitude, turbocharged Hercules VIII. Three built, converted to VI.

VI Long-span pressurised, with 1,600hp Merlin R6SM engines, no guns and special equipment. Used by 109 Sqn and as Gee trainers. Production 63.

VII One only, Merlin engines, tested large 40mm Vickers S gun turret for P.92 fighter, later with twin fins.

VIII Conversion of IC as Coastal reconnaissance version, with ASV radar arrays, Leigh light in long nose, and two 18in torpedoes or anti-submarine weapons. Some, huge hoops for detonating magnetic mines.

IX Conversion of IC for special trooping.

X Standard bomber, similar to III but 1,675hp Hercules VI or XVI. Peak production rate per month in 1942 was Weybridge 70, Chester 130 and Blackpool 102. Production: 3,804.

XI Advanced Coastal version of X, no mast aerials but large chin radome, torpedoes, retractable Leigh light.

XII Similar to XI, with Leigh light ventral.

XIII Reverted to ASV Mk II with masts, and nose turret.

XIV Final Coastal, ASV.III chin radome, wing rocket rails, Leigh light in bomb bay.

XV, XVI Unarmed Transport Command conversions of IC.

Total production of this outstanding type amounted to 11,461. After World War II hundreds were converted for use as trainers, the main variant being the T.10 which remained in service until 1953. The T.19 was a specialised navigation trainer. The Vickers successor to the Wellington, the bigger Warwick, was inferior to four-engine machines, and was used mainly in Coastal and transport roles.

Above: By 1943 almost all the new-built (as distinct from converted) Wellingtons were maritime variants with anti-ship radar, Leigh light (for seeing surfaced U-boats at night) and rockets, torpedoes and depth bombs. HZ258 was a Mk XI built at Squire's Gate in 1943, seen off the Cornish coast.

Below: This Wimpey from a Polish squadron had completed more than 60 'ops' (operational missions) when this photograph was taken in 1942. It might be a Mk IV, flown by Polish squadrons 300 and 301.

OTHER GUIDES IN THIS SERIES....

PRINTED IN BELGIUM BY

INTERNATIONAL BOOK PRODUCTION